S0-BFC-540

Wet Mittens

By Lorrie Bridges

Wet Mittens
By Lorrie Bridges

Copyright © 2014 by Lorraine E. Bridges
All rights reserved.

ISBN-13: 978-1496103802
ISBN-10: 1496103807

All quotations are from The NIV Study Bible, 10th Anniversary Edition
Copyright © 1995 by The Zondervan Corporation. All rights reserved.

No portion of this book may be reproduced, stored in any retrieval system, or transmitted in any form or by any means without the express written consent of Lorraine E. Bridges

Acknowledgments

During this long journey of writing my first book, I've had many cheerleaders along the path who got me to publishing. The first was my friend and author Nancy Kennedy, who gave me the nudge to just start writing! My father Eugene Marks held my hand and encouraged me to go after my dream before his death. My children Noelle & Chris Ritter, Whitney & Jeffrey Ernest & Grant Bridges deserve special thanks for asking me yearly if my New Year's resolution was the same, again?…to finish my book? My talented son in law Jeffrey Ernest created the book cover drawing so I wouldn't be forced to use a crayon drawing of my own. Many friends gently inquired how the final copy was coming along. Without a doubt my husband John Bridges deserves the most credit for cheering the loudest and insisting I keep writing. Saying a simple thank you seems insufficient for the love and support I've received. I humbly thank God for you all.

Contents

Introduction

Chapter 1: Humble Basketball Beginnings

Chapter 2: Month of Mom

Chapter 3: Fixed On the Unseen

Chapter 4: What I Wish Someone Had Told Me

Chapter 5: An E-Ticket Style Marriage Adventure

Chapter 6: Beauty College Capers

Chapter 7: Herb Flavored Friends

Chapter 8: You Gotta Love Deeply

Chapter 9: How I Became the Sex Mom

Chapter 10: Seasoned By Many

Introduction

I get some of my best ideas at 3 AM. Unable to sleep one night, I tried to remember one of my earliest childhood memories. I was four years old and living in Montana. There was snow. Lots of snow. Mountains of snow. Tunnels of snow. Playing in snow. Sledding in snow. Walking in snow. Shoveling the snow. When I finished my snow activity, I would come inside to thaw out and to begin the process of the removing all my layers of snow gear. When a large family of five children and two adults remove hats, boots, scarves, snow pants, coats and mittens you can only imagine the chaos! My parents had a few rules to maintain some sense of order. If you did not hang up your coat you might find it outside in a snow drift the next time you looked for it. I happen to know this from personal experience and can attest to my secret inner desire to not repeat that behavior! I lost count of how many times I retrieved my coat from a snow drift. Another rule was to hang your mittens by the heater so they would dry and be ready for the next time you ventured outside in the snow. I vividly remember learning the importance of this lesson. If you didn't hang your mittens to dry, then when you went outside again, those moisture filled mittens would freeze, making the whole snow experience quite miserable. You might say I started observing and learning about life's choices and consequences with my wet mittens. Thus began a lifelong process of learning. Learning by observing others in the game of life and I realized while playing in the game myself I now cherish often simple and profound truths.

I humbly offer to you some of my favorite and most memorable lessons. I hope you laugh, remember, and enjoy. You might even find yourself inspired to go out and make some new memories of your own.

Chapter 1

Humble Basketball Beginnings

"Be strong all you people of the land, declares the Lord and work for I am with you…my Spirit remains among you. Do not fear."
Haggai 2:4-5

My bible just happens to be open on my desk as I write today. The verse above seems to be beckoning to me for it is with much fear and trembling that I commence to write this short book. I am not very practiced composing my thoughts into book form. I fear failure. I fear rejection. I fear anything I write won't make sense or be communicated properly. I suppose the above Bible verse is a good place for me to start. I need assurance that this journey is not one I embark upon alone. This journey began a long time ago. The words, "You really should write a book!" have been said so often to me in the past 30 years that I finally decided to try. Worst case, I learn another life lesson. Best case, maybe I bring a smile, or ray of light into someone's life. Parting words of encouragement from my terminally ill father gave me the final shove I needed to begin this adventure. Squeezing my hand he whispered to me, "Write that book Lorrie."

So, I resolved to collect ideas, stories, memories, and life lessons to write about. From those earliest memories of lessons learned from wet mittens, to the time I really started appreciating and processing the lessons of life in high school, I have been blessed with many good mentors. Family, friends, teachers, and even coaches have imparted wisdom to me. Many of the lessons were learned from personal involvement…but others were learned while observing others from the sideline…while sitting on the bench if you will.

I am old enough now to begin to remember what I forgot. This amazing realization came to me one winter while attending my son Grant's junior varsity basketball game. It was half-time and all the parents were standing to stretch and console or brag and rejoice with each other about how our boys played during the first half. Most of the basketball moms had gathered and were chatting when I announced, to their surprise, that I had played basketball in high school. This was a well-kept secret that I had never shared with these friends. Their faces displayed varying degrees of shock, surprise, doubt, delight, and maybe even a hint of envy. You should know that I am only 5'4"; not your typical basketball star material! I ignored the open jaws agape and went on to tell a few stories of my high school years on the girl's basketball team.

Of course the first story was simply that I MADE the team. I do realize that I may have been the 15th member of the squad, but I MADE the team (so I had some skills to my credit). Well, truth be known, I was probably selected for the team based on my cheerleading background and the fact that I was generally a nice girl who wouldn't give the coach any problems. Someone must have told the coach he could round out the roster with me. I can't remember his name, but I do recall he was kind of cute with a fashionable moustache.

We were playing in a tough game against arch rivals and our starting guards were really getting worked over by a feisty girl from the opposing team. Controversial fouls and her foul mouth were annoying. Watching from the bench, I was agitated and internally begging to get into the game. Each time one of our players came to the bench they updated us about what we didn't see going on out on the floor. Ooooo we wanted "feisty girl" out of that game. The entire team was consumed with a chance to take her down. Then the nod from the coach came! It was my turn to relieve the starting guard. Whoa, I couldn't believe coach actually wanted me in the game. This didn't happen very often and I quickly ran to check in and play. Coach reminded me not to foul and to keep control of the ball. My heart was pounding as I guarded feisty girl whose skills shamed me. In my unfettered zeal I quickly had a foul called against me. Man oh man, this opposing guard *was* good. I assured the coach I was fine and that I'd settle down. Feisty girl was getting on my nerves as she swatted at the ball and breathed ugly speech in my face. It didn't take long for my sportsmanlike behavior to fade and my inner (and usually suppressed) bad girl to rise to the surface. Feisty girl was teetering on the out of bounds line and holding the ball looking for an opening to pass to another player. I was guarding her closely when I saw my opportunity for revenge. I just pushed her out of bounds with one hand and backed away as she lost her balance and fell. I still remember the shocked look on her face as she tumbled! How could I do that? I wasn't playing by the rules! How dare I push her? I was quickly called for another foul and I walked back toward the bench…a bench full of wildly *cheering* teammates and a coach shaking his head but smiling at me as he subbed me out of the game. I can't remember much else about playing basketball that day but I will never forget their faces and the feeling I had being in the game that day. I did it for the team!

I concluded my story to my adult friends and proceeded to tell them about the *only* time I was a starting guard player for basketball. Since this only happened once I remember it fondly. Our large school was playing a tiny school, in a "don't blink or you'll miss it" town a little north of us. They were dedicating their new gymnasium that day. A bazillion dollar gym that everyone had sold candy, washed cars and held bake sales the past 100 years for. Our junior varsity girl's basketball game would be the first "official" game played on this sparkling new court. I state no exaggeration when reporting that EVERY citizen of this small Montana town was in attendance. It was a packed house. The mayor, city council, founding fathers, mothers and school band with balloons and ribbons were all there. Imagine their surprise when our team spilled out onto the floor for warm ups with our faces marked with permanent markers from a initiation ritual doled out by our varsity team to the lowly junior varsity team on the bus ride to town. One by one we emerged from the back of the bus with decorated faces! I had large eyebrows and a handle bar moustache. I was truly thankful not to have the tic tac toe face that one girl had! All the junior varsity players had decorated faces in all colors and décor. I remember a tennis racquet face, and one with so many red dots she looked like she had measles. For reasons known only to the writers of the Twilight Zone my Coach decided to start me that night…why in the world did he pick that night! Was he getting even for my earlier antics in that memorable game against the opposing foul mouthed feisty girl? I didn't want to be in that gym let alone start as a guard that game! I desired to shrink away and not play. Despite my trepidation, I stepped up to play and enjoyed the privilege of starting. Looking back I realize that night was a once in a life time moment. I cherished that moment, smiled, waved to the crowd and didn't take myself too seriously that evening. I may have even forgotten that my face was marked up with a moustache. I am eternally grateful I had the opportunity to play basketball in front of every man, mother, mayor and child in that small town!

Chapter 2

Month of Mom

"These commandments that I give you today are to be upon your hearts. Impress them on your children. Talk about them when you sit at home and when you walk along the road, when you lie down and when you get up." Deuteronomy 6:6-7

Am I selfish? My musing started when I realized last fall that I don't really like sharing my mom with my siblings. Coming from a family of five children I'd been sharing her all my life. So during one of my, "I feel sorry for myself" moments, I resolved to invite my mom to come to California for an extended visit. I would plan a month of activities with her. After all, I told myself she *needs* me. It didn't take too much coaxing before she had the plane ticket in hand and planned her escape from the lonely house where my father passed away 10 months earlier. Little did I know that it was more about me, needing her. I started learning lessons the minute her plane touched down.

As I waited for her to emerge from the United Airlines gate my mind was racing. I saw my mother for the first time since she put me on a plane in Montana back to California after my father's death. Finally she rounded the corner jostled by numerous other passengers seemingly frantic to find their families. She looked good, though travel weary, and oddly the first thing I observed is that she needed a haircut (which I assume she saved for me because I used to be her hairdresser). I can't believe that's what I noticed first! I mentally made a note to myself to make time for that tomorrow. Then I heard her voice. I heard that familiar kind voice. I felt a pang in my heart and realized just how much I loved this woman and had missed her. I secretly prayed my teenage son would behave and my husband wouldn't regret having his mother-in-law visit for a month. I smothered her with greetings and we quickly headed off to dinner at a local restaurant. As we are seated I immediately got a call from my older brother checking to see if she made it safely and if we collected her? Sheesh, it had only been 20 minutes and he was already calling?! I still have to share her with siblings 1000 miles away! Later, I made another mental note to call mom more often and especially when she travels. After all, I can't be shown up by my brother.

I planned a ladies tea to honor my mom. I have been envious of my local girlfriends who get to do things with their locally living moms. So I decided to invite some of my local friends to do a local tea with my not so local mother. I have amazing girlfriends and about 15 of them showed up. Many of these precious women prayed for my mom when my father's health was failing and while she cared for him. There is a special camaraderie among women that men will never understand. We empathize deeply with those who suffer like we have. Loss, abandonment, and pain are just a few experiences that link and bond womens' hearts together…forever. I am eternally grateful for the girlfriends who came that day to "bless and honor" a woman who impressed God's commandments on my life.

We celebrated my mother Shirley that day over fancy china teacups and sweetbread. I surprised her by reciting some of the life events that made her such an amazing and remarkable woman in my eyes. As I recalled this simple woman with a simple faith, many tears flowed in the room that day. I reached out and took my mother's hand and told her how proud I was to be her daughter. These are the kinds of moments I had missed since we decided to make our life in California apart from our families in Montana. This was my loss. I purposed that I wasn't going to let one precious moment of our time together to be average, boring, mundane, predictable or lacking in sincerity. We all treasured our moms (living or deceased) at the tea that morning. I learned how much it cost me to raise my family several states away from their grandparents and our extended family. I felt the loss. But that morning I recovered some of it as I looked into the tear stained faces of my friends and we cashed in on love. Love from a daughter who dared to take a moment to appreciate and express honest thoughts about her mother. Not a privilege I have every day like my local friends do. Lesson learned? I would no longer hesitate to say I love you or hold back anything when it comes to otherwise loving my family and deepening relationships. Something tells me we all walked away changed that morning. Something tells me the biggest change was in me.

Over the course of 30 plus years of living a long distance from my parents hundreds of special events transpired that we never got to share together and thousands of everyday, yet important moments passed without doting grandmothers cheering from the sidelines. Finally on this visit my mother got to see her grandson run in his cross-country finals, she volunteered with me at the high school to help aspiring students learn the art of "interviewing for a job", we picnicked at the park with my husband, giggled through fortune cookies after Chinese food lunch, enjoyed tea and scones at the "Tuck Box" cottage tea room in Carmel, explored art galleries, and strolled the famous beaches of Pebble Beach and Pacific Grove. We packed a lunch and hiked in Point Lobos State Park. Those days are etched now in my memory. I'll never forget the image of my mom perched on the rocks at a point watching fishing boats drop crab pots while foamy surf crashed below us. My mom reluctantly fell in love with my turf, my home, and my stomping grounds…and I fell in love with her all over again as a grown woman.

We also took a couple of "road trips" as adventuring souls. One took us to her first triathlon experience in San Francisco. We stayed overnight with friends but had to rise early to get to the race site for her grandson and son-in-law to race. This meant she had to be up at 4AM. I went to wake her up and she was already fully dressed and bags packed! This was one amazing woman. I reminded myself that she was a hearty Montana gal and I should be proud I came from such admirable stock! Several noteworthy moments occurred that day that

made it especially memorable. Upon our pre-dawn arrival we met a
lovely lady from NBC who took our picture and put it on their website
that day…sorry if you missed us! We were also chosen to blow a horn
for a wave start of triathletes. Mom easily scurried up the 15 foot
tower platform ladder like she had been doing it her whole life. She
later said her skill came from all her years of tree climbing as a child.
The announcer interviewed her in front of thousands of participants
and spectators. Here's how it went…Announcer: "I understand this is
your first triathlon event Shirley, what do you think so far?" Doting
grandmother: "Oh it's just wonderful, but we did have to get up kind
of early to get here. I'm used to that though. I just pretended we were
going hunting in Montana and I was fine!" I looked around at the
neoprene clad crowd and bundled spectators who were smiling and
laughing. That's my mom… I just love her.

Okay, one not so glorious moment occurred shortly after her famous
speech to the crowd. After scampering down the announcer's tower
and briskly walking to view her grandson emerge from his swim she
stumbled and fell. Moms don't fall do they? What did she trip over?
Why wasn't I holding her arm? How did I let this happen? She had
quite the bump under her eye and I knew we needed ice. I'd been to
enough triathlon events to be familiar with the dreaded medical tent.
We found out later she was the only person treated that morning…well
that was just great! The swelling increased and a purple tone was
setting in under her eye as I told her she needed to concoct a story to
deliver to the questioning public. How about she declares she injured

herself at a triathlon during the run portion of the event??? My idea didn't go over too well. Good thing she was staying in California for a long time and could heal up before I sent her back to my siblings in Montana. Surely they would think I'd been neglectful of my mother and never let her return! We spent the day cheering for our brave triathletes as they transitioned from the swim, to bike, to run and then cheered wildly at the finish line where mom enjoyed the privilege of hugging tired sweat soaked bodies. As she recalled the events of the day she told us you have to remember "toes up" when you walk so you don't trip, as you get older. Now is this where I mention that her bruise blossomed into a lovely black eye the next day? Just in time for her eldest granddaughter's engagement party. Yes, she is a classic Montana gal. Toes up everyone!

We made another "road trip" to southern California to accomplish several other "first time" adventures. We stayed with childhood friend Dolly who had lived with my parents after high school during a tumultuous period in her life when she needed a safe place. That blessing of hospitality now came full circle as my friend, through tearful hugs, showed that same gift back to us. Sharing our home with friends or strangers was very normal for me growing up. My mom could whip up a casserole and bread with only moments notice. It was as if the freezer reproduced on it's own in mom's house! My own children are continually amazed when I too accomplish this feat. I guess it's in the genes!

My mother and I then visited my daughter's college campus at Azusa Pacific University in southern California. We were treated to a tour given by doting granddaughter Whitney who was so incredibly honored to show us around! We rode the "jolly trolley" to west campus and stopped numerous times for her grandmother to be introduced. Oh yes, I got an introduction too, but there is something special about having a *grandmother* on a college campus. Special meals shared and special moments etched. One such moment was when we attended the campus chapel service with Whitney and all her regulars. At one moment during the worship time I saw Whitney grasp the hand of her grandmother and they worshiped together with tears leaking down their cheeks. It would have been so easy to grasp my mom's hand and join in but I refrained and totally enjoyed the precious moment displayed between them. Life lesson learned? Love deeply. The rewards show up at the best time for your viewing.

We had more memorable times in the greater Los Angeles area with my mom's first "In-N-Out Burger" experience. We all watched her take her first bite and then witnessed the expected delight on her face. I wonder if this is the same way my mom felt when she experienced a first time event with me? Did she delight and giggle in her heart to see my face as I did hers? As a mother now myself I surely knew the answer to my own question.

We spent a few days for a "first" visit for my mom to my sister in law Robin's home in Murrieta. We enjoyed the family time, as Robin was once the recipient of my parents' hospitality in years past as well. Full circle once again…will it not ever end?!!! We attended my brother in law's church where he was the pastor of a large vibrant congregation. My mother had never heard him speak publicly. That day was special as Greg delivered an amazing sermon on turning your dead ends into detours. We listened as he laid out what God just might be up to when we reach those dead ends. I'm sure those words had special meaning for my mother who had recently become a widow and was well acquainted with grief and questions for God about her circumstances. It was a coincidence for us to be there that Sunday.

We had more adventure ahead as we spent an afternoon with my dad's adopted little sister Elissa and his favorite niece Melody, my cousin and their families whom I had not seen for 25 years. We shared a meal with lots of laughter and love sprinkled in with some tearful moments as together we remembered my father. A connection was made again with family. It strengthened my resolve to keep at this family connecting thing!

Mom and I made one more stop before returning home to the central coast of California. Not being familiar with southern California she asked if we were near where her cousin lived. Yes, we were! A quick call was made and a last minute trek put us on his doorstep! A visit to see her cousin Bill Smail in Thousand Oaks! Upon shaking his hand and taking one look at him I saw the remarkable family resemblance on my mother's side! I was with family!!! I was acquainted with the warm familiar Major laugh and demeanor. I listened as they spoke of the past. The family bible was brought out to check on some historic detail. My mother even submitted that reading God's word was helpful to her and encouraged her cousin to do the same. We chatted about our present lives and health challenges and the cancer that took my father's life. I was struck with the realization that this could be the last time these two might see each other. My throat swelled with emotion as I digested that this was a special gift God gave me with family. My family. My mother. My life. Another life lesson I learned was to never let distance hinder my relationships. Even though miles separated me from my family, I missed them, but hadn't lost their love.

Chapter 3

Fixed on the Unseen

"Therefore we do not lose heart. Though outwardly we are wasting away, yet inwardly we are being renewed day by day. For our light momentary troubles are achieving for us an eternal glory that far outweighs them all. So we fix our eyes not on what is seen but on what is unseen. For what is seen is temporary, but what is unseen is eternal." II Corinthians 4:16-18

I can still remember my friend Claudia's words during a phone conversation over 10 years ago. "Sit down, there is no easy way to say this...I have breast cancer." That began a journey in my life of understanding that I am still trying to comprehend.

Recently a friend told me he thought I had a special calling to help people going through the pain and challenges of cancer. I think he said this because I seem to have an overwhelming number of friends and family who have been afflicted with that disease. Maybe he is correct about my having a special gift though. The truth I have learned has been a huge blessing. After my father died of lung cancer I was finally able to see things about others I never saw before. When you walk with someone who has cancer you learn an awful lot. It's a painful...gift. Some things I didn't want to learn and would have never signed up for. Thank God He didn't listen to me and signed me up anyway. I am grateful that so far I have remained on the bench and haven't personally played on the court of cancer yet. I'm paying real close attention now to that game and to those in the "fast break" of cancer as we watch the seconds tick off the clock for them. It's been a surreal experience in recent years of losing so many I love to illness or a life cut short by tragedy. My lessons have been learned at their expense. These lessons I treasure most. They are my lessons of things *unseen*.

When you meet, shake hands and make a new friend you don't ever expect that one day you will hold them as they experience the loss of miscarriage, help them as they pack their belongings to move away from you, or tenderly caress their feet as they sleep through the ravages of a chemo treatment. I discovered extraordinary strength in those who were so weak from their treatments.

I took a chance and determined that I would draw myself close to my best friend as she courageously fought breast cancer for 8 years. Fear might have caused me to draw away, but love helped me stand near to the end. The lessons learned were so deep and personal that I'm still sorting through the "playbook" she left with me during our years of friendship. It revealed to me that people with terminal illnesses surprise us with their strength, stamina, sense of humor and eternal insight! I had to be brave with her as we treaded into unknown waters and an unknown future. Our conversations about her fears and cancer treatment were often easier spoken to me (a friend) than to a family member. I learned later she was really trying to protect her family because of her passionate love for them. Taking time to just "be there" was the lesson I had to be content with. I was folding a load of laundry, making a pot of spaghetti sauce, attending a doctor appointment, driving her to buy a scarf…and singing her to sleep when nausea was overpowering her. My dear friend taught me through dying, about how I was to live. I feel emotions so much deeper now and love with much more sincerity. The cost of cancer tore at my heart as I watched my friend battle, but the legacy she gave me created a vision to see with new glasses things unseen that God desired for me to see. I will be forever indebted to her for teaching me about real friendship.

If losing a friend wasn't enough…my father was courageously battling cancer in his life court. I was not prepared for what lessons were about to hit me with his full court press bearing down. I never believed my father would succumb to cancer. He was my dad, my protector, father of 5 children, veteran of 3 wars, a mighty hunter with guns, (from Montana!) the fixer of every small appliance (we rarely bought anything new as my dad would resurrect everything!), and car technician who repaired my 1977 Datsun with a Band-Aid on the highway once outside of Ulm, Montana. He couldn't die of cancer because he was much too tough and heroes don't give in to that disease! My mother told me that my father was the bravest man she knew. After 3 years of waging a war against cancer he lost, but he was the bravest warrior I ever saw in the fight. It was without complaint or fear that he set forth an example to me his daughter of how to live a life and live it with excellence no matter what cards are dealt to you.

When I finally accepted that his time was running out, I started planning a trip for my son and I to travel to Montana to go fishing. I desired for my son to learn how to fly fish from the master himself. We took their RV and boat up to the lake. After being out on the lake one morning and coming in for breakfast my dad and I sat around the morning campfire. He laughed and pointed over to my son standing on the shore practicing his technique. He wouldn't put that fishing pole down for one second to even eat breakfast! I could tell how proud of that fact my dad was when he said he had never met anyone who could out last him in fishing except that grandson! That proved to be one of the last times my father went out camping and fishing. Once again, it was another gift to us. I'm so thankful I sacrificed time and money and made that trip to Montana with my son to see his grandparents. Later my brother sent me my father's fishing license he found when cleaning out dad's boat after his death. Imagine our surprise when we saw a grade school picture of my son, dad's fishing buddy grandson, tucked inside with the license! That little tender side of my father showed his love for his grandson and how he took him with him every time he went fishing. He never was alone. He had our love and tucked it away in his pocket to remind himself.

Dad had a few "moments" during his cancer treatment that made us smile. As the lung cancer progressed to brain tumors the prescribed radiation caused hair to not grow on both sides of his head thus giving him a Mohawk type hairdo. I recall my mother insisting that I suggest a little trim before my daughter's high school graduation party to make it look a little more even and less like a tribal Indian chief. He complied since I was a former hairdresser. Then there was one of his final hospital stays where he decided he had enough treatment and was going to go home. Fearing he would call himself a cab and check out, my mother took his clothes and left him there with just a hospital gown. Upon reaching home she asked me to call him at the hospital and calm him down since his anger would indeed be great toward her. He was quite upset with her obstruction, and quickly surmised that I must have been talking to my mother and that's why I had called. I look back now and realize my mom turned to me because she knew he'd listen to…me…a daughter he loved. We also believe that the tones of my voice were still audible to his fast fading hearing. Another gift. I did calm the storm that raged and he went home a day later after the tests were done. He never returned to the hospital and accepted that his treatment on this earth was now complete until he went home to be with the Lord…where he would be completely healed. After the holidays I planned to travel and spend an indefinite amount of time as needed to help care for dad. Mother told me how he kept asking all day when I was coming from California to see them. He was becoming annoying as he kept inquiring about my estimated time of arrival! The sparkling smile from those blue eyes and hug I received when I arrived was a gift I will never forget. He allowed me to care for and feed him just as he once did for me as an infant when I needed him. He maintained dignity and humor until his final hours. I remember him rolling his eyes at me while catching my attention, as mother and I would discuss various topics in his presence. He'd wink at me and tell me what a wonderful daughter I was. We laughed about Jell-O jigglers and pretended to toast with them in the air as we ate them. He was the one who I dared tell that I wanted to write a book one day. He reached for my arm and pulled me toward him and said, "You write that book!" I saw how loving and tender he and my mother were toward one another in their final days of marriage. I learned that I didn't want to wait until my final days to show that same tender love I saw displayed to my own husband of then 25 years. I'm starting today to be tender toward him. My father held my hand one day and kissed it over and over and told me he loved me. What child doesn't desire that expression of love?! Ah yes, another gift. I was privileged to be with my parents the night my father passed from this life to eternity. This was a special and holy moment that will haunt and be cherished by me forever. This journey to temporal death death surely is a two edged sword. It just plain hurts, however, the lessons bring comfort and healing to the soul. The unseen things for me are still being discovered. As Claudia always said, "God is in control." Later, I would say, "God is enough." I think I prefer it both ways.

So many lessons learned…holding the hand of Nancy, my friend who was a recent widow and now breast cancer patient as her hair was being shaved off as she exclaimed, "I will never ever complain to God about my hair again!" Later when long time cherished friend Kerri was going through chemo for breast cancer, Nancy gave me a blue wig to send to cheer her. I learned to love bald women whose natural beauty isn't dictated by curls and bangs stylishly placed around their faces. My friendship with Kerri also taught me that you drop what you are doing and make time to visit a friend going through cancer treatment. I also sought courage from 19-year-old Riley and his family who bravely lived out their faith like none other I have experienced before in my life as he endured bone cancer. My sister in law Robin had a 2-year list of various surgeries, complications, disease and frustration before being told she had thyroid cancer. I learned to hold her hand, cry and pray like I never had before. I had faith that an understanding of the pain and suffering of those around me would one day come to me, if not in my lifetime here on earth then surely in heaven! Recently my girlfriend Shelly fought breast cancer as a single mom and I assured her I wouldn't let her face it alone. I also learned from Ada, Diane, Dana, Jane, Sally, Lois, Susan, Dick, Roland, Jackie, Alice, Luwana, Matt, Fred, Jill, Linda, Binky, Becky, Dixie, Ted, Larry, Jenny, Renee, and Barbara. You all taught me more about being on the field in the big game than you'll ever know. I guess I learned a huge lesson of loving through the hard times. Something tells me if it's me someday I won't be alone either and your faces will show up on my doorstep with just the right expressions to teach me about unconditional love and friendship. Hmmm, maybe another chapter in my next book?

Chapter 4

What I Wish Someone Had Told Me

"These commandments that I give to you today are to be upon your hearts. Impress them on your children. Talk about them when you sit at home and when you walk along the road, when you lie down and when your get up. Tie them as symbols on your hands and bind them on your foreheads. Write them on the doorframes of your houses and on your gates." Deuteronomy 6:6-8

Almost 30 years have passed since I first became a parent. I don't know if I believe that qualifies me to give advice since I'm still learning the art of parenting my adult children! I think I will continue to gather advice just to be safe! Recently while watching a sporting event at my son's school, I asked 2 girlfriends for advice on how to handle a situation with him. Other moms are wonderful for that information! I still feel as much like a rookie parent today in some situations as I did 29 years ago when our first daughter was born. True confession: I called the pediatrician to find out if my daughter could sleep with the pacifier in her mouth and not suffocate. Halleluiah, she still lives today to laugh about it with me. I could regale you with stories about my many new parent blunders but instead I've decided to discuss the lessons I've learned from the bench of parenting. The limited help I had in the early years required me to turn to God often as I knelt on my knees and exclaimed, "Jesus, help me!" Oh, a few books here and there have been helpful, but nothing beats learning the old fashion way of being in the trenches and performing on the job training for the real deal. How I longed to have someone…anyone, give me a few "tips" to aid me along the way. So here it is folks, my parenting from birth to adult tip list that I believe has had a positive impact in raising my children.

Never stop learning and keep trying to improve and build upon that which you've built. May you and your family be a continual "work in progress!"

1.   Be pro-active not re-active.

2.   Teach the 4 D's.

3.   Understand the importance of peer groups.

4.   Keep them doggies rolling, & have FUN!

5.   Don't neglect your spouse. Keep that relationship #1.

6.   Employ consistent age appropriate bible study.

7.   Prepare dating guidelines for your children.

8.   Place the bar high.

9.   Teach consequences.

10.   Don't give them everything they want.

11.   Circle the wagons!

12.   Teens need genuine care & balance of parental talking with listening.

#1   Be pro-active not re-active.

I think this is number one on my list because I always seem to come back to it for all my children in all situations. Simply stated…be ahead of the game and be prepared for it. Be good Boy Scouts and follow the motto, "Be prepared." Anticipate! Here is an example to help you. All of my children separately thanked us for discussing with them privately the topic of sex and how babies are born **before** it was deemed necessary by the public school. They were grateful to be "in the know" and not have that deer in the headlights appearance their friends all had when receiving that information for the first time. Just endure some eye rolling and visit the topic frequently. Be assured they will thank you later for not reacting to your fears and being too slow or inattentive to see their need for the facts of life. I heard it once said, "To fail to plan, is to plan to fail." You need to stay current on the youth culture and hot subjects in the media. Get some resources and be ready for your teenagers on every topic!

#2   Teach the 4 D's.

These 4 D's were not tolerated in our house: **D**isrespect, **D**ishonesty, **D**isobedience and **D**iscouragement. They apply to **all** members of the household. This accountability with one another is fruitful for better attitudes and behavior in your home. We talked about them all the time and the best policing behavior took place when they would catch *us* as parents breaking one of the 4 D rules. We also taught our children the *opposite* 4-D's ...Respect, Honesty, Obedience and Encouragement. Ok, one moment to brag here... for a time our local paper ran a column about families. We submitted an article and were photographed and put this into print about 15 years ago. Without a doubt it was our 4 D's comment that received the most feedback from readers in the community. Four little D's can have a BIG impact.

#3   Understand the importance of peer groups.

I recall a conversation I had with my daughter in middle school. We had observed a young man walking on the sidewalk with his pants sagging to his ankles. I casually asked, "Do you find that style of dressing attractive?" My daughter said she did not. I remember being quite relieved. Another time we attended a college graduation for a close family friend and reclining several rows in front of us was a young man who was covered with various radical piercings. I asked my daughter what she thought of his style choices. She said she didn't care for it and wouldn't bring him home to mama! Can you imagine my relief!!! My biggest fear was my children's choice of peer groups in school. We decided to use them to our advantage rather than be paralyzed by them. Here's an example: My husband coached our daughter's softball team for the purpose of facilitating her friendships with other children who were kind, loving and similar to our family's moral beliefs. The team he drafted didn't win the league title but some of the relationships my daughter formed have endured to this day. Peer groups can have a powerful influence on your child. As they grow into their teenage years they become even more important. As a parent you must actively sacrifice so you can create easy access for your child to maintain and nurture positive friendships. Your own healthy relationships will serve to show them what to model their own after.

#4   Keep them doggies rolling, & have FUN!

We are an active family. If you aren't one, then you just need to change today and become one. We never allowed our children to own a video game center. If our kids wanted to play video games it was at their friends' houses, not ours. We preferred to hike, bike, explore, & do family adventures TOGETHER. Like Christmas tree lightings, parades, craft fairs, cultural festivals, concerts, dog shows, and local sporting events where you live! Later they would bring along friends, college roommates, & boyfriends (now **you** can check **them** out!) Our kids would ask us all the time what we were doing on the weekend?! Our outings became affectionately (and famously) known as "Sunday Adventures." We always had something planned as a family and kept the little doggies rolling constantly along. Recently my college-age daughter re-read a first grade writing journal she kept. She had written about all the family activities we shared over the weekend when she wrote on Monday mornings in her journal. She exclaimed, "Mom, we did a lot of really great adventures when we were kids!!" Boredom was never spoken of in our home. If you did, the activities director (me!) would find you something to do!! My husband and I were on a trip last spring when I suddenly turned to him and said "We're fun!" Seriously…we have fun together and do FUN things. This has been contagious to our children. I love it when we just drop what we are doing and add in the fun factor.   Fun people do fun things and attract other fun people or aid those less fun to have more fun. Get it? One day I told my kids I was taking them to do something fun. We got in the car, went to a park, bought ice cream on the way home, and sang songs in the car. Be a FUN parent…your kids will want to spend more time with you!

#5   Don't neglect your spouse. Keep that relationship #1.

Our oldest daughter was 2 weeks old when my mother left to go back home to Montana following the birth. I remember my husband & I cried since we were now on our own and scared to death. I recall one evening after nursing a colicky baby that I finally had empty arms to hug my husband. I hadn't done that since before the birth. It had been 2 weeks since I had hugged or touched him. We both held each other and promised to not let the baby ever come between us. Continue to date through those infant & toddler years. Attend a local marriage conference. Making time for your relationship is of utmost importance. Try a little event such as a beach walk or a quiet conversation in the wee hours of the morning. Here's a lesson I learned from the bench watching others in the game of parenting…I've seen too many marriages where one parent put the relationship with the children first and eventually the marriage ended. Now, 34 years later as the empty nest approaches, I have not forgotten all the reasons I married and madly love my man. The best thing a parent can do for their child is to love their spouse and keep that relationship fresh. Children "watch" and learn so model for them what real love looks like.

#6   Employ consistent age appropriate bible study.

It's the little things they will remember. They won't recall the expensive and time consuming organizing it took to plan that trip to Washington DC. No, they will remember jumping on the hotel beds and drinking orange soda and having orange tongues and laughing loudly till someone got in trouble. My husband faithfully read a children's bible to our 3 young ones every day while he was preparing for work during his shower & shave time. All of our children remember this activity more than anything else! They'd join him in the bathroom for their daily routine, dragging along their favorite blankets and toy bears to learn and listen too. Make time for AWANA, youth group, Sunday school and regular church attendance. These experiences stick with them a lifetime.

#7   Prepare dating guidelines for your children.

Our oldest daughter was the catalyst that prompted our formal adoption of some family dating guidelines. She was a freshman in high school when she came home and announced a boy with whom we had been acquainted since 2nd grade had asked her to the homecoming dance. You really think you are going to be prepared to embrace dating and relationships for your teenager, but frankly, you aren't!! You are totally freaked out. My sweet husband huddled with me in our bedroom that night and with hushed tones asked me, "What were all those rules on dating that we've been formulating for years anyhow?" The next day we (together with our daughter), found ourselves hammering out boundaries and formulating a roadmap for her dating years which included many of the items and terms that we'd been discussing since we first held her in our arms (we deleted reference to using guns to fend off inappropriate suitors…that only pertains in Montana). We agreed, and wrote down what would become known in local circles as the "Dating Guidelines". Since we had already discussed our expectations for dating and marriage with our children long before it came knocking at the door, teenage dating wasn't all that bad. Secretly I believe our children were thankful for the guidelines. We tweaked them once or twice as unforeseen circumstances arose. They served our family really well. If I had charged a $5 every time I copied or discussed them with other parents we could have paid for a semester of college education!

#8   Place the bar high.

This thought is really quite simple and can be summed up with a surfing phrase I heard once, "Go big, or don't go at all." I love that all out abandon to doing the best ever, or expecting the best ever! I always taught my kids to do their best and nagged them with "any job worth doing is worth doing it well…" Often they were re-doing the job to a higher standard. I told them they should expect excellence and strive for the top mark. It should be noted that I was NOT the scholar student when I was younger, but my husband was. I learned this lesson actually from being married to him. I suppose if you walk along side someone for the years we've been married you start to adopt some of their patterns of thinking. This has indeed been one of them. I found this most important when talking to our children about not settling for second best in their relationships and to be the best friend they can be to others. We found that placing the relationship bar high also tends to weed out people who don't genuinely have your child's best interest in mind. Those people who are too lazy or don't want to work at a sincere relationship give up and move on thus helping your child to recognize true friends and solid relationships that will stay with them for a lifetime.

#9   Teach consequences.

I taught the topic of abstinence and sex education to teenagers for 9 years in local area high schools. (That is another chapter all on its own!) A quote we often used and wrote on the board for discussion was, *"You are free to choose to act, but you are not free to choose the consequences of your actions."* There are positive and negative consequences to every action we choose. As a parent you can show and demonstrate the wonderful consequences we reap when we choose to obey listen and love cheerfully. You can also lay out the consequences that happen when we argue, disobey or act in an unkind manner. There always needs to be the awareness that a consequence will transpire…and you must then insure that it does.

#10   Don't give them everything they want.

My husband always wanted a dog growing up. I always wanted a flute. Neither of us got the beloved item we longed for until later as adults we got a dog and my girls serenaded me with lovely flute sonatas! I also thought I needed a pony but thank God my parents had the sense not to buy me one as I am not what you would refer to as a " horse person". What was I thinking? When our children were in elementary school we implemented a unique program for them and soon discovered we built in all sorts of life lessons we didn't plan on! We gave our children TV watching coupons when they were quite young. Each coupon was worth 30 minutes of sitting in front of the "tube" for entertainment. This included movies they were allowed to watch as well. They each had their own envelope so we could manage their accounts (and know if any cheating was going on). We allowed them to offer another family member a coupon out of generosity if they desired to share. If they had coupons left over at the end of the week, then we would let them cash them in for 25 cents a coupon. Oh, it didn't take long for them to learn to save coupons for Saturday morning cartoons, or a special movie with a friend. Our middle child made a bundle of money when she discovered she could just as easily play rather than watch TV. Her piggy bank filled up fast! Our young son learned to calculate how many coupons it took to watch an episode of Sesame Street. Our two girls decided they wanted me to buy "The Little Mermaid" video that had just come out. We said they could buy it, but with their own money. We instantly became the evil parents who wouldn't buy them the video EVERYONE else in the world owned! We did not budge and those 2 girls didn't watch TV for 3 weeks and pooled their money together. I happily took them to buy the cherished video when they earned it. Oh yes, the good old-fashioned way (as a bonus, we let them watch it for "free"). We still talk about the "TV coupons" and the positive lessons about life learned from that simple exercise. Budgeting, planning, saving, charity, and resource management were among the lessons learned. We just stumbled upon this creative method that was complete with incentives!

#11 Circle the wagons!

I really don't want to say, "It takes a village to raise a child," so I say, "circle the wagons" instead! Back in pioneer days the covered wagons traveled westward with all their earthly possessions. During attacks from the local natives they would circle the wagons for protection and provide safety for their families. Be sure to circle your children with other individuals in their lives beside yourselves as parents. They will tire of hearing your voice spout out directions for life and soon you will be a monotonous sound to their ears. Allowing others to participate in loving and nurturing them is a benefit I can't place a price tag on. Recently one of my son's friends referred to me as his "mom" on his Internet Facebook page. What a compliment that means so much to me! Invite your youth pastor, neighbor or adult friends to join the wagon train with you.

#12   Teens need genuine care and balance of parental talking with listening.

I have not found one teenager who disagreed that caring and listening to them were absolutely the most important things to them. Sometimes we talk too much as parents. We are desperately trying to impart our wisdom to our children knowing the precious few days we have with them are slipping away. We don't really listen to their hearts crying out. We are too busy, too bothered, and too tired from raising them to listen...really listen. I dare you to go ask your teen if caring and listening to them are important to them. Ask if you talk too much and listen too little. If you take time to do this you will hear and remember that young teen of your earlier years shouting out to be heard and acknowledged. Care enough to listen. Listen and you'll discover what care is needed.

On the other hand, some parents are afraid to talk to their kids. As teens get older they try to separate themselves from you and try out their own wings. We seem to think it's okay to not talk to them. I have numerous friends whose teenagers talk to me and not to them! Why is that?! I know facts about my friends' children that my friends don't even know or suspect. It really doesn't need to be that way if you establish the communication line early and don't let the train get off track. Here's an example, my son would be angry about something and say, "I don't want to talk about it!" "That's fine," I'd respond, "but eventually we **will** talk about it." When tempers cooled and the emotion from the disappointing baseball game or drama from a junior high friendship had subsided we would ALWAYS talk. They learned to expect it whether they liked it or not. Talk, talk, and talk to your kids! The biggest challenge is finding the balance between knowing when to talk and when to zip your mouth shut and STOP talking.

Chapter 5

An E-Ticket Style Marriage Adventure

"We love because He first loved us." I John 4:19

March 15, 1980 began my E-ticket ride with my husband John. When we got engaged John told me marriage with him would be like an E-ticket ride! I think I was supposed to be very impressed and totally won over by him with this comment. John was a bit taken aback when I casually asked, "Uh, what's an E-ticket?" For those of you who never visited Disneyland before 1982 and only know the famous theme park with its present day one price admission for all… apparently in the old days the "best" rides at Disneyland required an "E" type ticket to ride them. Dumbo and Pinocchio were an "A" tickets, while Pirates of the Caribbean and the Matterhorn were "E" tickets. Well, I married John before ever visiting Disneyland and our adventure began.

Recently, when our best friends' son was announcing his upcoming marriage I pondered what great wisdom I could bestow upon him. I told him marriage was a life long adventure. I knew he wouldn't get the E-ticket part since he was too young but I think it sums up how this marriage ride has been for us. We have learned a Disneyland amount of lessons while married. It has been a Small World after all when we got our first married student housing apartment. Though most of the time it is, there are days it hasn't always been The Happiest Place on Earth. I now live in Cinderella's castle on the beach in California! Funny thing, one of my husband's nicknames for me is Beauty. I love it. I just need the hair and the dress now! Fortunately I don't need to call him Beast very often. The lessons learned during marriage with my Prince Charming have truly helped define much of who I am today.

Just days before our 20th wedding anniversary I answered what would be a memorable phone call after delivering my 3 children to school. I don't remember everything that happened in those moments but I will never forget the sound of my husband's best friend telling me of my husband's bicycle accident. He was very afraid. He said I should come right away to the site of the accident. I didn't admit it until years later but I purposely and calmly took the time to change my clothes before rushing out the door. I'm not sure why I did that. I would've expected any normal person to grab their keys and break all speed records to get to their loved one. Instead I composed myself and began what would turn out to be a very difficult day of my life. Maybe I instinctively knew that I wouldn't be changing clothes for a few days. Within the hour in the buzzing ER room the doctor soberly informed me that my husband had broken his neck at the C-2 vertebrae. My brain was flooded with more questions than answers. I suddenly realized I was making decisions for the two of us and not just myself. In our marriage vows, we declared in sickness and in health and for better or worse. We were staring down the worst moment of our married life. Miraculously, God "caught" him that day so he wasn't paralyzed (as most C-2 breaks result in that). It would be six months to a full recovery, including a unique surgery, painstaking physical therapy, much prayer, and truckloads of patience to heal him. He is a walking miracle! I should probably write an entire book about the experience and what I gleaned amid that struggling time in our lives. For now I will just share one incident that stood out in my mind.

John required full-time care for many weeks, which included bathing. We set up a special chair in the shower stall and I helped him into the stall to be seated while I bathed him. While I kneeled before my usually strong in control confident husband and washed him carefully I noticed that he was crying. Uh oh, what was wrong? I asked if he was okay! He tearfully admitted that he didn't believe he could bathe and care for me like I was doing for him. He tearfully added and asked how could I do this for him? I almost burst out in laughter as I placed the washcloth on his feet kept washing him and said, "Well, I'm a mom! That is how I know how to do this!" I reassured him that he could do this for me if it was needed someday. I knew right then that I had married the most honest loving man ever when he admitted that he didn't know if he was capable of providing such care for me. He was so vulnerable during that whole time of healing which gave our marriage a new dimension. It's hard to say who changed more during that tragedy in our life. We were both radically changed forever.

Two of our three children are married now. Friends and family ask me if it was hard to "give them away" in marriage. I have a simple answer for that. It's not hard if they are marrying a God fearing and remarkable individual who completes them. The best day of my life as a parent was the day my oldest daughter got married. Oh, I did have a few anxious moments several days before when I panicked and inquired if I had done enough, taught enough, said enough, (I'm sure she would of said YES to those questions) and lastly…did I pray enough? I calmed my inner fears and assured myself that my job was done and her future husband was an exceptional man of character I could trust. I learned just recently how much that young man cared for my daughter when she became seriously ill with the flu. She required immediate transport to the hospital for care he couldn't provide. He called us early in the morning and asked us to pray for her and then later kept us informed as he took her to the ER and checked her in. He gave numerous updates as to her condition and care throughout the day and later let us talk to her on the phone as she recovered to calm any concerns we might have had. I told him that through those kinds of adventures it caused me to love and trust him more. A remarkable person makes a remarkable mate and marriage partner you can trust.

I do have a few personal marriage absolutes I've gleaned after walking down the aisle 34 years ago. I'd like to share my discovery with you.

- I don't return lumber. Guys, are you hearing this? Really honey I don't and won't. I told him it's just something I can't bring myself to be his helpmate with. Graciously he has accepted this absolute.

- I should have written into our marriage vows that <u>reciprocal</u> hand and back rubs are required. I often give but don't receive. Interesting thing is my husband feels the same way about this one but we can't seem to get it right.

- We make a game of who gets to perform the most annoying tasks for one another. We play odd or even and the loser has to let the dog out, get a late night snack, get socks when our feet our cold, answer the phone or do a chore. I'm always even and he's the odd. Appropriately chosen and named. I think I win 90% of the time.

- Do not buy me an appliance for any occasion without FIRST clearing it with me. True story...he bought me a crock pot for my birthday before we were married and actually said out loud when I opened it, "Do you even know what YOU can cook for ME in a crock pot?" I should have handed him back his precious E-ticket right then and there and said "ride alone".

- Make "I love you" be your daily first and last words said to one another. My parents had a little bear on their bed that would speak those words when you pushed on its paw. A little lesson I learned from an old married couple of 52 years.

- Help out the brain dead spouse. Often times we can't recall the name of someone we've run into in public. If I don't introduce my spouse right away it is his cue to jump in and rescue me by sticking out his hand and saying "I don't know if we've been introduced before, what is your name?" We use this little trick a lot the older we get!

• Designer games! Years ago I received an email that described a fun loving way to surprise and communicate with your loved one. It's called "SHMILY", from the acronym - See How Much I Love You. We hide this little post it note size piece of paper that the other loved one has to find. I think we've been passing the same tattered one inch square post-it note it back and forth for maybe 10 years now. I even laminated the original paper! I have hidden it in funny places... Wallet, bike helmet, and even in his jock strap! I've also found it in some amusing places…inside a book I hadn't read for awhile, cosmetic bag and with the coffee beans. It's been a delightful game we've played for years. Love surprises me. It surprises me that I can still be deliriously in love with the same man for 30+years. It surprises me that with all the extras (gray hair, pounds, and wrinkles) I've added over the years my spouse still finds me the most amazing person he's ever met.

• Laugh! My husband thinks I'm quite entertaining for the most part. I must say I can be quick witted and have been known to produce laughter out of my friends at unsuspecting times. I'm no standup comedian but I've been told I am a funny gal. Nothing pleases me more than when I remark about something that causes my spouse to burst into a giggle. See, he doesn't have to laugh, but yet he does. I love that we laugh and have fun. John will often throw his head back and chuckle and say, "You amuse me!"

I suppose we never really appreciated how much we love marriage until the nuptials of our children came knocking at our door recently. I wasn't prepared for how difficult it was for my husband to "give away" his first-born daughter in marriage. I kept an email he sent out to family and friends who couldn't be there to share in the happy day. It was detailed, poignant, and filled with daddy love. See through his eyes how we felt that special day:

Dear friends,
John compiled some reflections from our daughter Noelle and Chris's wedding last weekend. I added a few MOB-mother of the bride-thoughts (in brackets). Enjoy...

Family/Friends: The wedding of our sweet Noelle was an absolute, 100%, complete, success!!! Things could not have been more picture perfect, from the bride and groom, to the "mother of the bride"- and her pink shoes, to the grandparents from Montana, to the smiles on everyone's faces. Having never experienced a wedding from the "front row" before, I wasn't sure exactly what to expect, but it was one of the most blessed days of my life.

The Friday afternoon rehearsal was a bit "uncertain" (as they always are) but we got through it all as the bridesmaids were in puddles of tears during the rehearsal which was anything but a "dry-run" through with all the crying!

We then headed off to a wonderful luncheon hosted by Chris's father Larry. All were just a buzz with anticipation about the coming day's events. We enjoyed greeting all the out of town arrivals at our hotel (many of us stayed at the same place in a cluster of rooms together) and we all then joined with friends for a fantastic dinner at a nearby restaurant. It was fun to hear every comment about whose cousin and family member looked like each other. Most questions were, "Is that really John's brother?" and "She sure looks like her mom"! Noelle joined us and positively glowed the whole evening. One great moment was taking a picture of John's sister Robin (who caught Lorrie's wedding bouquet) and family friend Don O'Hair (who caught the garter tossed by John) at our wedding. Don was the only non-family member at the dinner that was also at our wedding 27 years earlier!

We arose "dark" (as opposed to "bright") and early on Saturday to begin the pre-event preparations. It is amazing how much time can be spent fixing hair and dresses etc...let's just say I was glad to be a male. [Yeah right...]. We arrived at the church early to help set things up and greet people as they arrived. The church was simple yet elegant. Noelle had done a masterful job decorating... [Just like her]...simple yet elegant. The groomsmen and bridesmaids were hustling around here and there but the bride was cool as a cucumber. The funniest things happen that you would just "never" think of. For example, one of the "issues" that arose had to do with passing around car keys to various vehicles. So many logistical decisions regarding transportation became almost funny. Oh yes...and the borrowed- - drive away car --"Porsche" keys went through many hands before finding their way into the groom's pocket.

The ushers (that would include the brother of the bride (B.O.B.) Grant) had a bit of a challenge getting everyone seated. It seemed that almost everyone arrived at precisely 10 minutes before the wedding time. But...somehow...they got everyone seated and we started only a few minutes late...but no one cared as all were being entertained with a wonderful slide show sister Whitney had created showing the classic "then and now" pictures of Noelle and Chris. One of those tear jerker kinds of shows...I purposely avoided it (trying to keep the tears in check.)

[I, the MOB never saw the slides either as I was in the hallway greeting people and hustling about. But I soon realized seeing all these precious loved ones made me cry. I could not turn off the happy tears and had to retreat to the hallway! One comical moment was when we barricaded the doors so Noelle could come out and use the bathroom before the ceremony. We soon realized only the men's room was available so several bridesmaids held & protected her dress so she could enter in but not before Uncle Greg warned her of the conditions of most men's bathrooms! We all shared a roaring laugh.]

*Lorrie, Noelle, and I had a few moments alone just before "the walk"
during which we prayed together. It was a very special
moment. Again, the MOB was crying her tears of joy.
Finally the big moment had come; all but the bride and the FOB (that
would be me...Father of the Bride) were in place. As the groomsmen
entered, each of them gave Chris a "big" kiss on the cheek. They were
all chuckling together big time...Chris endured with good humor...but
his <u>focus</u> had not yet entered the room.*

*The entry music was a piano rendition of a song I had written 17 years
earlier for my sister Robin's wedding to Greg. Noelle had been a 6
year old flower girl at that event and to her, that song, Storybook
Love, always equated with wedding...so she wanted to walk down the
isle to it. It was quite an honor for me that she would choose that
song. I was overwhelmed by the moment...I felt kind of numb as we
walked...and blind (due to all the camera flashes)...probably a good
thing as I couldn't "dwell" on the reality that this would be my last
walk with my little girl...as my little girl.*

*After giving her hand to Chris at the alter I then sang them a song I
had written for the occasion. "Tears of Joy". The music was the same
as for the song I had written for Noelle when she was born. I stayed
focused on Noelle while I sang and fortunately she held her composure
so I was able to likewise...at least until the last phrase of the song
when I could no longer hold back the lump forming in my throat. But
all in all not bad compared to what I had feared/expected.*

Finally I was able to join "my" bride and watch the ceremony from the safety of the pew. [The big question asked later was, "How did you make it through that song without breaking down John?"]

Then came a moment none of us had anticipated. It was the tenderness of the foot washing ceremony. Oh my goodness…what an amazing symbol of love (see John 13:1 -- the "full extent" of Christ's love for us). Not a dry eye in the building (including mine). We then experienced an amazing sermonette from brother-in-law Greg Sidders…one that will "never" be forgotten by anyone. A fun word picture about lawn sprinklers and the "blessing zone" that will live in my mind forever…you'd just have to be there.

Then the kiss…the introduction…the standing ovation…and off we went to the reception at the Arden Hills Country Club.

Noelle had selected the venue and it was "way" more than I had ever expected. Again, perfection.

During pictures, the cake finally arrived (a whole story in and of itself that I'll share some other day) (let's just say we decided "not" to tell the Bride about the "missing" cake…)

Fun announcements as the wedding party entered. A few touching toasts, including one by Grandpa John offering to be a Ritter-sitter if

Noelle and Chris would hurry up and give him a great-grandbaby. And a funny story from Whitney the S.O.B. -- you can imagine the story... we changed her acronym to M.O.H. - maid of honor! Lots of laughter and joy spilled out over the whole celebration.

Then the father-daughter dance... Now that was a surreal experience to be sure. At first Noelle and I thought we were the only ones crying...during the dance but then we looked around to see "numerous" wet faces like ours.

As I locked on Noelle's perfect gaze, I could not think of anything but her and our many "father-daughter" moments together (sheesh I'm tearing up just writing this). :)

It was like one of those Hollywood movie moments where the camera circles around the couple...I was just floating there, laughing, crying, remembering, praying, holding her tight, thanking God for such a wonderful daughter and such a blessed life. I will never be able to fully understand that moment...not that I need to...I just want to relish it in my memory...forever.

Then the "fun" dancing began (and ended too soon). Every time I looked around the bride and groom were smiling and having so much fun with everyone in the room.

Then the new Mr. and Mrs. ran out of the reception hall through millions of tiny bubbles and raced away in the Porsche. Mother Lorrie got the last kiss to the cheek of her little girl which almost 23 years earlier she kissed as she breathed her first breath after birth.
Good bye...my love...my special girl...the joy of my life...my diamond from heaven...my pumpkin/Charlie Brown girl

If you ever get to marry off a daughter I can only hope that you are as completely blessed as I was (and we were.) Thanks for sharing in our joy.

John and Lorrie (aka FOB and MOB)

Who would have known that 2 years later we would be in wedding mode again with our second daughter!? I again saved an email I sent out to family and friends to capture some moments we savored that blessed day:

Dearest family and friends,
Over a week has passed since Whitney & Jeff married one another. Such incredible joy was in my heart that day. I tell everyone it was a lovely mixture of tender moments of tears and memorable times of laughter. They planned such a nice event to celebrate marriage. We are so very proud of them and it didn't take much to convince us that we love and adore Jeff as a son. Grant now has cool brothers out of the deal with 2 marriages to his sisters and we get these amazing

young men who cherish our daughters and fit right into our ragamuffin gang we call the Bridges family. There were so many moments before, during and after the wedding that are impressed on my heart and mind that I thought I'd share a few with you.

Whitney did such a good job preparing that we really had little to do the week prior except go out to lunch, bike ride, sit in the spa, walk on the beach and entertain friends and family. Really...she is amazing. Our close friends Rob & Lisa spent several days with us prior to family arriving and said they couldn't believe Whitney was making **them** *breakfast one morning. It was so relaxing and FUN! The hard work of organizing paid off in full return as we thoroughly enjoyed our loved ones and each other. That is my big tip to other mother of the brides...plan & organize, way in advance!*

The day Jeff arrived in Pacific Grove I saw a change in Whitney. The look in her eyes was bright...it's really going to happen! She just sparkles when she is with him. All you have to do is spend 2 minutes with them and you see how much they love each other. I thanked one of the best men (there were two!) for delivering the groom safely. The bachelor fun began and I swear they didn't sleep much for 2 days as they enjoyed "man time" which involved barbeque with a lot of meat, taking over the Cameron's house, beach bonfires, and late night convos and wafting evening cigars. These guys really love one another and it was great to witness. The girls did more refined activities with manicures and a girl party with a dozen or so gals having a playful time under Noelle's leadership as Matron of honor. Family and life long friends began to arrive at our home. It was quite surreal as the whole event unfolded before us with love overflowing. These two have done an amazing job of surrounding themselves with remarkable people who stood with them as witnesses to their vows. I felt like life went into fast-forward when the wedding day arrived. I must tell you I kept my emotions intact until Roland & Joyce McNulty arrived. Then I kept getting misty eyed a lot as Roland was best friend to my father while they served in Vietnam and having them here was like having a part of my dad and an extra set of grandparents to enjoy. They made it so delightful.

Let's not forget to mention that photo ID was needed to gain entrance to the reception on the military base that is home to the Naval Post Graduate School in Monterey. Noelle discovered late the night she arrived that she had accidentally left her purse (and ID) in Sacramento...God always has the details covered and her boss just "happened" to be coming to Monterey the next day and he delivered the purse to the forgetful Matron of Honor who almost missed the reception. Whew...that was a close one. A nail biter that would of ruined my nice manicure for the wedding!!!

The timing for everything on wedding day was flawless. The weather was perfect for photos and it warmed up nicely at the church. Whitney told me earlier that if everyone "cheerfully" does what they are supposed to do it would all go smoothly! It did. I sighed in relief when church decorations were complete, appetizers arrived and flowers were gorgeous as ordered. Whitney was calm and stunning and Jeff was handsome. We all cried as Whitney came down the aisle with John...Grant cried the most which made us all cry more. Whitney's grandpa John had a tear stained face and quivering lip that I won't ever forget. Flower-girl Kassia (age 2) realizing that she ran out of flowers half way down the aisle thought going back to gather as many as she could off the runner was a good idea. After a minute or so and oblivious to 250 people coaxing & laughing- Jeff came down the aisle and scooped her up and carried her the rest of the way. So sweet! 4 beautiful flower girls that were "mini brides" and needed a license to be that cute!! 12 Year old Jonah Silva played the processional like a pro to Pachelbel Canon in D. That was a big WOW moment for everyone. More tearful moments when John sang a song he wrote for the couple "Four Words" (I love you more). He barely made it through the song and not a dry eye was in the church! Their vows were so amazing and special as they put so much thought and effort into the words they were saying before God and men. Even Uncle Greg who officiated the ceremony choked back tears of love for magnitude of the moment. Brother in law Chris led the couple in communion and prayer and Noelle sang effortlessly while playing guitar making it a complete love fest for the ages. Prayer with parents led by both fathers put the final blessing and then a dipping kiss and whooping by the bride and groom as they were ushered out for a receiving line with hugs and smiles. The groomsmen took off their jackets and had signs taped to their backs describing their respective availability as they left the stage which gained lots of applause. Limited availability, Available Mon- Thursday, I'm taken, and one cell phone number! (I'm told he had calls all night long at the reception!!) I told you it was tears AND laughter!

The reception was so lovely...the 50 foot ceilings and 1920 architecture was perfect. Both best men, Matt & Eric, flipped Noelle in her dress as she was introduced by Chris (MC for the event) as his smoking hot wife! Noelle startled all of us with her gymnastics! The roasted chicken dinner with bacon, spinach and artichokes was exceptional! Cupcakes were served after the bride and groom danced and Whitney managed to over throw her bouquet beyond the waiting maids to a ...man! Uh, yes we did a re-do! College friend and recently engaged friend Laura made the catch. Best man Matt caught the garter. We all danced and laughed. I drug my brother Ken out on the dance floor and nephews Sean & Brian for a spin of wedding dances. We all had just way too much fun! One regret we had was that we wished we had allowed more time to visit with all our guests. Whitney and Jeff left in a borrowed Porsche filled with balloons to begin their long awaited honeymoon trip to Maui. Jeff squealed the tires and ran a stop sign as he left! The whole day just went by too fast, but I savored every single moment. My favorite was when Jeff and his mom were dancing and Whitney sat down next to me and said..."Mom, it has been a perfect day, thank you." Gulp...I grabbed her hand and smiled since I couldn't talk without crying. What a special day...what a special daughter and new son in law! We cried, we laughed, we cleaned up, we fed the 5000, we paid the bills, we changed the sheets on all the beds and then we began to enjoy this new chapter of two married children and the 2 new sons in law we just love to pieces. A perfect day. Perfect bride and perfect couple. God is so good and faithful.

All our love,
Lorrie & John

Here are two letters that poured out of my husband and me. We dared bare our emotions and spared no details of what was happening to our hearts. We desperately desire for our children to succeed and enjoy their marriages and we are confident they will. The marriage covenant is forever. This thing called marriage is weighty stuff! It tugs at your heart and changes you... Even as we married off our children, marriage was changing us. We were facing an empty nest with new challenges ahead. Gulp. Why wasn't I paying better attention during the ride? I took that E- ticket from my husband and hung on tightly. I look forward to hanging on and loving deeply for another 34 years.

Chapter 6

Beauty College Capers

"Indeed the very hairs of your head are all numbered." Luke 12:7

My early fascination with cosmetology may have begun with the "pixie" haircut in the 1960's. It might also have been because I remember my mother cutting my bangs using hot pink "hair tape". It came on a roll like gift wrap tape (and often was used to wrap birthday gifts when the regular scotch tape went missing). It would hold down my slippery straight blonde hair while she carefully trimmed with kitchen scissors. I do remember watching my father cut my brothers' hair with the dreaded buzzing clippers in the garage. Dad and my brothers would look like little clones with their matching "butch' hair cuts. He would use the same clippers on the family poodle too! We should have named that poodle Butch! I recall Dad would take me along when he got his hair cut at the barbershop. My husband remembers seeing girlie magazines in the corner of the barbershop waiting area. Funny how I don't remember that! There were never women or little girls in the barber chairs back then. Just overweight middle aged men in white smocks with slick sticky hair that winked at me. We girls went to the "beauty parlor" or more often, our mother would perm, cut and style our locks at home to save money for our family which had a tight budget. For those of you who didn't endure this memorable experience, let me give you the details.

Getting a home permanent wave was an ALL DAY affair. The strong ammonia smell would clean your sinuses out for the year! In the late 1960's the solutions weren't as advanced as they are now. I would get skin burns from the strong chemicals in the solution which would result in hair that would break at the scalp. Weeks later new growth sprouted that I didn't realize I had damaged. That made for a popular new look in junior high school! I endured hours of sitting and waiting as mother artistically wrapped my slippery hair with various colors of rollers. I remember growing weary of the ordeal and wiggling a bit too much and mother gently whacking me with the rat tail comb and pleading with me to sit still. I would see my older sister giggling at my discipline under a nearby portable hair dyer. My older sister only endured one home *Toni* permanent wave that I can remember. She must have hated it. I know she resolved to never undergo a perm again because she grew her hair out after that until she was in her mid 20's. She was smart. She never had to deal with bangs, curling irons, gels, or, our beloved mother cutting our bangs too short. She did have gorgeous hair to her waist. Her hair would turn heads and I overheard many conversations about her hair. I thought it was amazing hair .She had patience to grow and manage her gorgeous locks. I did not. I instead experimented and played with backcombing, pageboys, Dorothy Hamill wedge cut, bi levels, Farrah Fawcett layers, and permed curly hair. My wispy blonde hair would never grow like hers. I think I was destined to become a hairdresser as I searched for the perfect "do" for myself.

If you practice something long enough you can perfect it to a certain level of acceptance. I had been "practicing" haircuts on my college friends for almost a year. Everyone was fully accepting my novice abilities and the price was right…free! Hey, hey, now, I'm doing a pretty good job on these coiffures! I wondered about a career as a cosmetologist! But most of my so called clients were men. How would I get them to set foot in a beauty shop? I was certain I'd found my professional calling. I presumed my charm and delightful personality would certainly cause a stampede of customers begging for my talent. After some serious soul searching I decided to apply and attend Beauty College instead of my university pursuits. I had no clue that I was about to launch myself into a new world of creativity that would require me to manage and interact with all types of people. What I was about to learn would shape me for the rest of my life.

I entered Mr. Mack's Beauty College in Bozeman, Montana in January of 1979. There were 2 other Lori's already enrolled. Since my given birth name was Lorraine they requested I use Lorraine to cause less confusion with clients making appointments. I secretly knew my mother would be thrilled. I didn't mind my name but only recalled hearing it when I was in trouble. I always cringed on the first day of the school year when the teacher would do roll call in each class. They would call out your legal name and all your friends would laugh and snort hearing it said aloud. "Lorraine Estelle Marks…?" "Yes, I'm here"…heavy sigh.

So here I am again hearing my name said aloud thinking maybe, just maybe, I was done with that chapter of my life, but no, I wasn't. I needed to find a new way to embrace using the name Lorraine and get over myself. Besides, Lorraine sounded more grown up and mature. My friends and clients began to call me, Lorraine. Done. Mr. Mack also liked the sound of my name, Lorraine! French and classy. Yeah, baby that was me!

2600 hours of teaching & practicum at Mr. Mack's was required to complete this certification. A state board testing would complete the license. Full time for almost a year and you could sneak in extra hours on Thursday nights to speed up the process. Tips and an outside job were my only sources of income. I did all the math and calculations to realize the tough year ahead I was facing. I was so excited and confident though! Those first weeks introduced many new friends and experiences I will never forget. Sadly, I've only kept in touch with one of those girls but I cherish that we have (Carolyn Scott).

We spent the first month cooped up in a mannequin room wrapping perms on fake heads with various lengths of hair. Each time we finished a wrap it had to be checked by an instructor and crossed off a master list each student had to complete before moving to a station on the main floor. We also had to "set" with rollers varying styles which to this day I'm certain they only use in the morgue for casket preparation…more on that later. So for several months, I only "observed" actual haircuts. I never got to cut real live human person type hair until I completed the required hours with our silent, no fuss, mannequins. Those mannequins were sure compliant clients. We could whack them with our combs and brushes (a technique I had previously learned from my mother), gossip with them for hours, complain to them about our exams, never look them in the eye (plastic eye that was), pull their hair as hard as we desired, back comb a rats nest into that "up do", laugh at our end coiffure result and make fun of them publicly while drinking diet cokes all afternoon. Ah yes, those were certainly the days.

Finally the much hyped and anticipated day came for me to set up my station on the beauty college main floor and begin work with breathing homosapiens. My first day working on the floor was spent marking all my belongings with my initials "LM". That afternoon the giddy receptionist told me I would be receiving my first haircut client. I sat in my barber chair nervously fiddling with hair rollers and rehearsing my best smile for my first victim…er…customer. My sparkle clean white uniform was ready but I wasn't. They finally called my name over the intercom, "Lorraine, your appointment is here". I bounced up to the waiting area to meet a young dark haired boy about 11 years old whose hair desperately needed a smart new cut. He couldn't answer any of my questions about what he wanted and he didn't care. His mother had sent him against his will with cash in hand.

Oh dear…they were not going to be happy with the outcome I was quite sure. I insecurely worked my way through that hair cut for an hour while he sighed impatiently with my needless rechecking of my less than adequate abilities. I wasn't happy with the result but didn't know what else could be done. I just wanted this first hair cut to be over! "Cut Check!" I called out and Mr. Mack arrived with haste to my station to educate me on the spot as to my work. "Well, not too bad Lorraine" he said as he snipped and repaired the hack job on my poor boy victim. Mr. Mack showed me how to use the clippers to trim his neck and maintained his chipper attitude about the whole first haircut ordeal without giving my secret away that he was my first haircut. As I escorted him back to the cashier and then to vanish out the door, I only remember 2 things: 1). He didn't leave me a tip, and 2) I prayed I would never ever see him again in my life because the haircut was so bad. God has a funny sense of humor because about 10 days later and 35 more haircuts under my belt, I saw that boy again. I was horrified as I recognized him standing in front of me in line at the drug store. I examined every inch of his haircut as I stood behind him. I was so angry with myself for allowing him leave my chair with such a horrible hair cut. I was embarrassed. I vowed to myself that day I would NEVER NEVER NEVER allow a client to leave my chair if it wasn't a personal best. I wasn't humble enough to admit that first day on the beauty college floor that it was a train wreck of a haircut. I wasn't honest with the client. I should have swallowed my pride and got it right the first time. Lorraine was going to live her life with a standard of excellence that was going to be higher. That was the life lesson I learned that day. I wish I had that young man's name so I could Google him and apologize. I'd give him his money back too!

In my short (but seemingly never ending) year at Beauty College I learned many things about myself and others.

1.   I could talk to anyone about anything…anytime! Except the one man client who had 2 bandaged up forearms and informed me that he had cut himself…accidentally…with a knife. I was cheerfully cutting his hair and quizzing him on how he could cut himself on **both** arms accidentally when I suddenly realized he had tried to commit suicide. Our conversation abruptly ended and I hustled him out the door with a very short hair cut that wouldn't require him to be near sharp objects for awhile.

2.   Everyone's hair is different and you often know your hair better than your cosmetologist. We need to continually remind ourselves that we are fearfully and wonderfully made by the Creator. One client of mine insisted his hair grew slower on one side over his ear so he requested that I *please* not cut it there. If I did it would take up to a year to grow back. I reluctantly listened and complied and 6 weeks later he happily returned to my chair as someone who would be one of my most loyal customers.

3.   Women will sometimes lie to you about coloring their hair and their age. I never figured out why. So, to the older woman who colored her hair and lied to me… I am sorry I used a perm for the wrong hair type and your scalp burned and your hair fell out. I would be willing to

bet you don't lie about THAT again! Thank you Mr. Mack for loudly chewing her out (complete with expletives) and rescuing me that day from what has given me nightmares for years. I will always remember seeing those little perm rods with her hair wrapped around them lying in the sink after we quickly rinsed her out to stop the processing and scalp burning. Those dozen or so patches of bald scalp that would need to grow back still scare me!

4.   Straight blonde hair is the most difficult to cut and I had personal knowledge of that with my own golden locks. Thank you God for all the blonde jokes my family has kept me well stocked with.

5.   Learning to cut hair on a baby/toddler was a handy skill I would need later while chasing a moving target with my own 3 children. A minimum of 2 adults is required to accomplish this task. Tears and small bits of hair are very itchy and annoying. A small child hair cut can only last a few minutes before the "client" must be held down by the 2nd adult. Use whatever method/bribe is necessary to finish the job; candy, singing, cookies, a special "treat", candy, soda & more candy. Be sure to take pictures for the baby book before cutting that first precious lock. Occasionally the whole first haircut adventure goes awry and the "after" photos must be abandoned.

6.   Evidence in a brown paper bag of what your cat did to your hair was very convincing to me. One of my "to her waist" long haired clients tearfully showed up sobbing and told me a tale of her beloved cat chewing off her braid during the night while she slept. She brought the braid in the brown paper bag to prove it! She cried the entire time I cut and permed what was left of her hair. For several hours she sobbed

as we created a new identity for her. I just wished there had been a way to glue that braid back on. She left with the 24" braid still in the bag when we finished. Odds are she got rid of that cat!

7.   Some people are just plain…well…odd! In the early 80's nobody wore their hair short on purpose unless you were in the military. Military installations were nowhere near the Beauty College so I was confused when a silly young man came in and told me he wanted his head shaved all the while yakking it up with me. Let's just say I didn't believe him! I told Mr. Mack he wanted his head shaved and I didn't know how to do that. Truth is I didn't want any part of that kind of hairdo! Mr. Mack playfully took the clippers and gave him a Mohawk and then after we were done giggling shaved the remaining portion. We were totally entertained that day with that young man treated as if he were a mannequin!

8.   Good news travels fast. I was surprised and totally overwhelmed one weekend with an engagement ring I received from my fiancé John while in school. I didn't tell anyone the news and decided to wait and see which girlfriend would notice my gorgeous marquis style diamond first. I don't think it took but 30 seconds for one of the other Lori's to notice my new engagement bling! I won't forget the shock on her face and asking me if I now leaned to the left side when I walked. To this day I love to hear good news first!

9.   Work hard at anything and you will eventually be rewarded! I put in the "extra hours" on Thursday nights during Beauty College so I could finish sooner. I graduated first and I had a job lined up with a former instructor at the school who desired my styling flair and work

ethic in her newly opened salon. You never know who is watching you. I still like the name of that salon, The Hair Surgeons.

10.   Beauty College provided some colorful tales but mostly it produced confidence and creativity that carried me far in my personal life. When you work with people daily, you can agree with me that there isn't anything that surprises you. I felt equipped and ready to be licensed to practice cosmetology, but I learned so much more in that brief stint at trade school. It prepared me for a life of interacting relationally with people from all walks of life, men & women, young and old.

11.   Life stories are to be shared and re-told! Mr. Mack told us some real whoppers about when he worked nights for extra cash at the local morgue on dead clients! We would roar with laughter hearing his tales of bodies emitting sounds and only charging "half price" since it was only the front around the face he styled. He said the customers never complained. He loved to tell those stories of his with a twinkle in his eye. I think I may have learned the joy of story telling from him while in Beauty College! That may come in handy some day as I repeat these adventures and capers to my grandchildren.

Chapter 7

Herb Flavored Friends

"A man of many companions may come to ruin, but there is a friend that sticks closer than a brother." Proverbs 18:24

My high school boyfriend Herb asked me at a high school reunion, "Why did we break up? I can't remember, do you?" No Herb, I don't recall. At the time it must have been a BIG deal to both of us but now, all these years later, I can't remember the reason. As we chatted at our 30-year high school reunion I was more interested in what kind of dad he was. How was his marriage to classmate Debbie? Tell me about your life! Update me about your sister I played softball with. Did he know how much I admired the way he handled all the teasing we dished out to him by calling billiard cue sticks…"Herbie sticks" (because he wasn't much taller or wider than they were)? To this day my own children call them Herbie sticks! It suddenly came rushing back to me though. I do remember one huge thing I learned while dating Herb. We had **fun** & we **laughed** a lot. Somehow while navigating the waters of dating I learned that important lesson and tucked it away in my pocket and saved it to remember when I met the man who became my husband. I wanted to have fun and laugh like I did with Herb. Years later I had Herb to thank for that lesson. Now John makes me laugh & we have fun together. We should all take a little "Herb" with us into our next relationship! I was learning that a little bit of those individuals I loved and cared for deeply as a boyfriend, girlfriend, roommate, co-worker or neighbor, were tagging along with me whether I liked it or not. Friends from my past shaped much of who I am today due to interactions and divine moments together! What an epiphany to discover this truth and to begin to remember what I learned from various old friends! I spent time identifying some attributes that I received over the years. Got me thinking…hmmm….should I change their names to protect them or honor them in this chapter!?

At that same 30 year high school reunion I found myself face to face with the young boy (now a man) who gave me my first kiss. I was so happy to see him after a 30 year silence in my life. I cried when I hugged him and told him I always wondered what happened to him and didn't know if he was dead or alive! The strong emotion of care and concern overwhelmed and…surprised me! I was jolted back to reality when Herb then mentioned that I had dated all 3 of the men standing there with me…gee thanks Herb… "who kissed the best" he asked? Oh no! We were heading toward the junior high boys locker room in a hurry so I put an end to it by proclaiming that Blake had been my first kiss! This admission was news to my old beau. His name had often been blurted out of the mouths of my children when they were feeling feisty and desiring to tease their mom a bit. I hadn't planned on him hearing this family guarded information in the first 5 minutes of our grand reunion. He was so popular and athletic and I was certain he had more "experience" than I did in the smooching department. Tales had been told to me about his reputation with the ladies of North Junior High School. So my first formal dance and first kiss all rolled into one night I will not forget. Elton John tunes and an evening of slow dancing. I learned so much from that first relationship. I learned what it felt like to be special and desired by the opposite sex. Getting all dressed up for the prom and making myself all pretty was fun. Of course young infatuation faded as it always does and Blake and I quickly learned we were not very compatible. I learned not to dwell on someone I knew I wouldn't have a future with. I also learned that you never stop loving someone. It was a different kind of love that I would later have for my husband and children. My heart surprised me with its capacity to save a secret closet of care for those early relationships that I would build upon for future ones.

You never know when a former boyfriend may resurface in your life so you had better remain friends. Ask any of my children how many times when they were dating I would remind them of the story of Jeff. One of my best life lessons involves him as the first boy to ever give me flowers. I met him at church and we dated for several months. He actually was the best boyfriend I had ever had. This blue-eyed handsome blonde turned out to be more of a brother than a boyfriend. It broke my heart to end the relationship but I still have him in my life years later. After breaking up he surprised me several months later with red and white carnations on Valentines Day with a simple note that said," love Jeff". He taught me so much about love in friendship.

It has lasted us our entire lives as our families have intertwined over the span of 35 years. Because we remained friends I met and became best friends with his older sister in college and he would later live as roommate and become best friend of the man who became my husband. It is a funny world. Later my husband and I would sing at Jeff's wedding, our children became friends and years later his wife (and close friend of mine) would joke on Facebook that I kissed him before she did. This precious relationship taught me to keep the bar high when it came to choosing a husband. He modeled for me what a healthy loving companion should look like. I will always love him for the life long impact he has had on me.

I did have two blind dates... thanks to my older sister Cheryl for the first one. He was a life guard buddy of her boyfriend. I thought to myself, can't be all bad if he's a lifeguard. The look on my conservative military butch hair cut father's face when he came to the door to pick me up with his shoulder length hair covering his dark eyes should have been my first clue not to go out with him. A night not to forget as we watched the hit movie Jaws. At least a lifeguard could save me from the angry shark! The second blind date and what would be my last blind date was in a small Idaho town for prom. I was visiting a friend and she set me up with a boy who was popular, drop dead handsome and available. I had my suspicions why he wasn't taken but took a chance and said yes as his date. My date was the epitome of a "gentleman". I felt like Cinderella all night long. What a sweet experience and memory that was for me. Not until I got married did everyone in the room keep their eye on me like they did that night! Thank you Gary for modeling that gentleman and prince like quality so perfectly that I recognized it in my husband when I met him.

I hope everyone had a little "Wayne" in his or her life like I did. Wayne was the boy across town from "the other" high school that I dated for 6 months in high school. He was a handsome gymnast who had muscles on his muscles. This young freckled face boyfriend companion escorted me to my high school Homecoming events, fun dates, numerous church activities and camps. We had many late night conversations in his light blue VW Bug! Aw, good times! The most important lesson I learned from Wayne was that he taught me to just… be… myself. I could so easily do that around him. He was the most comfortable easy going guy ever. I had just begun dating him when I met John (who would later become my husband). Wayne was concerned that John was flirting with me by begging me to play tennis with him. I assured Wayne that we were only friends and that he had nothing to worry about. I recall telling him I would NEVER date John. Years later in college Wayne would examine my engagement ring and ask me again about not dating John! Hey, I never said I wouldn't marry the guy! Recently we reconnected via social media and it felt great to catch up on our lives. I'm so thankful for the loving pure relationship that we had that helped me… feel free…to just… be me.

It has to be mentioned that my older sister and I actually dated not one, but two of the same guys during our high school years. Imagine the look on my beloved boyfriends' face when my rough necked father would answer the door (as he frequently did with our dates) and chat it up with them before asking which daughter they were taking out on a date? "Who are you here for, Lorrie or Cheryl?" It wasn't my dad's first rodeo...he loved to make those boys squirm.

The list of those who flavored, seasoned, spiced & peppered my life is long. Many are worthy or mentioning.

I've been blessed with a mother and father in law who have treated me like a daughter for 34 years. By their example I am attempting to accomplish the same goal with my children's spouses. I also named my son after my close friend's son Grant because I loved the name she chose (means: generous heart). My friend Peggy said the boys can grow up and be friends...and they did. Friends share things, even the name of a child. My friend Laurie who knows and loves me so completely can read and tell if I'm distressed just by the sound of my voice! My sister in law Robin calls me the sister she prayed for. My childhood friends Dolly, Darci, Sheila, Melanie and Steph guard secrets about our junior high and high school years that we will all take to the grave with us. I am totally surrounded by loving individuals who are effective in making me flourish with their love and season every part of my life. If we stop, pause and reflect we will appreciate the wealth we have in the love we share with others, past and present. The recipe for this lesson learned has been passed down to me. I'm gonna go spice up someone else!

Chapter 8

You Gotta Love Deeply

"...And I pray that you being rooted and established in love may have power, together with all the saints, to grasp how wide and long and high and deep is the love of Christ..."
Ephesians 3:17-19

I was back in my childhood home with my husband visiting my parents. We had arrived late so we were sleeping in like slug-a-beds. Not sure what those are but I'm pretty sure they don't move fast and they need coffee in the morning. I remember lying in bed and just listening. I was listening to the house wake up to the morning. It usually involved my father's coughing and familiar throat clearing and then his proverbial footsteps to the bathroom, the flush, the pipes shuddering, more steps, the dog whining, the back yard door opening and shutting, cupboards creaking, and more coughing and steps. It was the sound of the coffee maker dripping that I remember, not the usual sensory smell of the coffee. It slurped loudly beckoning me to join my dad for coffee and if I looked pathetic enough he would make me breakfast before trying to coax me outside for a predictably windy day in Great Falls, Montana. If you listen...the sounds of your childhood family home will echo back to you. My children will remember customary house creaks (especially that last step before the stairwell landing), birds, sprinklers, and garbage trucks. Whatever those sounds may be I didn't notice how intense they were until they were absent the morning after my father passed away. I swear I heard him cough and walk down the hallway like usual, didn't I? The coffee maker roared to life, not by his hand but by my own. Those sounds were a warm blanket to soothe me for years to come. It is those sounds I desire to stop and reflect upon that taught me many lessons. It was those childhood home sounds I purposed to mimic in my own home. I love to see my adult daughters stumble out like a pretty slug-a-bed to join me for coffee and breakfast. Those conversations and quality time are precious gifts to me.

I now hear the sounds and echoes of years past from when we raised our children in our home. "Performances" were almost a nightly entertainment fare after dinner. We'd see dances, gymnastic jumping, ballet leaping, and wild artistic movement from our 3 children in the living room. Some I captured on video, but most were captured in my heart and soul. Have you ever walked through a room and seen your child in a familiar over-sized costume flash before your eyes!? I have! I've seen my infant son toddle past the corner of my eye in what my husband fondly called "the wall scraper" a.k.a the infant walker. I testify that I hear them singing made up songs and whispering from their rooms. Those rooms have since been transformed into lovely theme decorated guest rooms, but the echoes are forever.

Fast forward and I hear from my son after his second year of university…"Mom & Dad, I want to go to India for 6 weeks next summer." Not exactly the words I was expecting to hear. I was thinking more along the lines of, "I will really need to get a job at home this summer!". I think I went through all the stages of grief and kept coming firmly back to <u>denial</u>! Well, maybe he would change his mind and move onto something else? In the past he had changed his mind like he changes his socks so there was still hope! Maybe a girl would distract him!? Who goes to India besides our pastor and Mother Theresa? Surely this too shall pass…but it didn't and the daily ache in my heart as I prayed for him while he was on his missions trip to India is a reminder of what rooted long ago when I first found out I was going to be a mother in 1983. Trusting children to the Lord's care isn't always easy.

My friend Donna is newly pregnant with her first child. We chatted on the phone for an hour about how she's feeling, the changes to her body, her fears and plans. Is it a boy? She thinks it's a girl. I assured her she'll be a wonderful mother. She's trusting blindly that she will be able to succeed at this "*mothering thing*". As we converse I am reminded of how I felt emotionally when I found out we would be parents. Transporting back in time I recall my obsession with how everything I ate would affect the baby. I learned all I could about nutrition and eating spinach and green leafy vegetables for extra iron. I became an avid reader about prenatal and child development. My new goal in life was to now provide, protect and personally take charge of this child and keep her from harms way…forever. During the pregnancy, delivery and first weeks after her birth I was consumed with her welfare. Any blemish, rash, ear infection, childhood disease became cause to stop the earth's rotation until I solved it. Split ends and bratty middle school girlfriends would suffer my wrath if they messed with my precious offspring. Young courting boys would suffer much trepidation at the hands of my husband, but also had to endure my watchful mother's eye if there was any hint of a bruised heart. My default mode was to handle, manage, nurture and care for my 3 children. I never discontinued that mode.

India was looming in the distance and my son would be extremely out of my reach and watchful eye. I couldn't use the default mode for anything! Suddenly I was blindsided by my fear of an unknown and possibly hostile culture. As I was telling Donna she will be forever changed as a mother, it dawned on me that all my worry and concern for my adult son was wasted energy as I could do absolutely nothing for him while he was on this 6 week adventure serving the extreme poor, dying, and destitute half way around the world. Suddenly I missed him…a lot. You see, when he left for college it took me almost 6 months to finally miss him. My husband and I were too busy having fun redecorating the empty nest and flitting around town without the baby birdies!

Now that I'm thinking clearly and have settled into the grief "acceptance" level…my heart loves deeply for him. I'm so thankful he's in India, not Indiana. He's following the path God has directed him to. Reading his short emails were salve to my mother's heart that missed him. His team partnered with a local church to help feed 10,000 people…daily. He writes of needing patience with a young boy that he aids with his writing skills. He tells of assisting a dying man and how the man moves slowly…even his eyes. He says the man's eyes are filled with gratitude as he lifts him back into his hospital bed. My son says it's hard but he's learning so much. I now understand that it's so very good for developing the gifts he has that are just waiting to be revealed. These learning moments would likely not happen under my supervision and watchful mothering eyes. I fought the default mode of keeping him out of harms way. I soaked some Kleenex tissues. I cried out to God Almighty to care for him. Maybe this India trip is all about helping this mother amend her old ways of protecting to her children and adopt new ways? Shortly after that crying session I received an email from a friend whose son just left for Iraq for 8 months. Sigh…my self-absorbed soul anguished for her instead tending to my own selfish pangs. I still have such a long road to travel in my journey of life, but I will never apologize for loving anyone too deeply. Technically his college degree is in Business Administration but in so many ways he graduated with a degree in life (shout out to Azusa Pacific University). My transformed heart makes me a grateful mom as I see him begin his life's flight. I love him so much that I have finally been able to put my selfishness aside so he can soar.

Awhile back I almost finished this book. But after seeing the great cathedrals in Europe and learning how they took hundreds of years to build, I decided to give myself a little more time. When I later received a phone call from the hospital declaring my older sister's leukemia diagnosis I informed my husband I would never finish my book. I was far too distracted to carve out time to write my thoughts down when they are so consumed with concern for my sister. Another chapter could be dedicated to the past several months alone. As an avenue of release I became the blog writer on the Caring Bridge to inform the family/friend masses of my sister's journey through this complicated blood disease. Even if it's painful and bids adversity we can come away with lessons. Maybe the herb seasoning I've acquired has "stuck" to me because I allowed it to. My sister Cheryl and I talked long one evening and decided we were thankful in the midst of her medical challenge. Thankful we didn't need adversity to say the things we want to say to one another. We already had done that in calmer moments of our lives when one of us wasn't being tossed about in the storms of life and leukemia. We had a peace between us that surpasses understanding.

While visiting our oldest daughter one weekend she told us about the frightening loss of a client who died suddenly of a heart attack and collapsed at work. He was a sweet favorite of hers and the loss surprised and impacted her young spirit. Thereafter she seemed more than usually attentive to us (her parents). As we were driving away after the weekend together she stood outside their apartment waving to us. Not something she frequently did. It was the *look* on her face that gave me pause and I flung out my arm for my husband to stop the vehicle at once. She came running over to the car with tears running down her face. I asked why she was crying. She said, "I just love you both so much!" I hugged her awkwardly through the car window and with tears now pouring I clearly understood her fears. I said, "It's okay to love deeply. That is the best way. Don't apologize for loving that way!"

Sniffing back the emotions we managed to drive away. It was obvious to me that I had successfully passed the ability to love deeply along to my first born child. There isn't anything better than a love that reaches into your soul and tattoos itself there into eternity. May you live your life deeply and contently as you love, laugh, and learn.

Chapter 9

How I Became the Sex Mom

"Whatever is true, whatever is noble, whatever is right, whatever is pure, whatever is lovely, whatever is admirable- if anything is excellent or praiseworthy- think about such things."
Philippians 4:8

Marks-a-lot, Groucho, Blondie, Stellish (thanks Robin), Lor, Pistol (my friend Rick calls me) and Lovely (my husband's favorite) are just a few names I have collected over the course of 54 birthdays. Of my many unique nicknames "sex mom" was one I never would have imagined for myself. I have a young man who was working at the local REI sporting goods store one day to thank for that most surprising title. He nervously eyed me as I made a purchase during the busy Christmas season. I smiled and questioned how we might know each other, but I suspected I already knew the answer for I had previously encountered numerous teenagers in similar situations. Speaking with a low tone and leaning over the counter toward me he said, " I believe you spoke in my health class to me, aren't you the sex mom?" Oh dear! I never saw that coming. Couldn't I be the "sexy mom" instead?! I did throw my head back and laugh and claim that I had never been called *that* before. As I stepped away from the register I asked if he remembered anything I taught him that day in health class? A few facts and stories had remained with him which made me feel successful as I drove home anxious to try out my new nick name on my family.

I'm not quite sure what prompted me to volunteer at the Compassion Pregnancy Center and to become a public speaker to rooms full of hormone raging teenagers. My curiosity led me to observe Debbie, a veteran abstinence educator friend of mine who was speaking at a local high school. She was quite funny, comfortable and confident as she selflessly poured out information to the pubescent crowd. I wondered if I could actually stand in front of strangers and speak so casually about such an intimate topic. Since I didn't have blossoming teenagers in my home quite yet, I wanted to see her presentation and check out the local action. My friend encouraged me to sit in the back of the class and observe. I discovered that I was quite comfortable in a room of 30 students casually talking and interacting about the topic of sex. Most people would have run screaming out of the room in fear. Teenagers don't scare me like they do other people so I stayed and sat through the presentation all day never once having the urge to bolt and run. Instead I found myself drawn in and believing that I too could possibly become an abstinence educator to our local public and private high schools. I started taking copious notes and privately delved into my personal past so that I could begin to formulate my own presentation. With my mentor's help, I quickly found myself regularly presenting to teenagers. One of the first lessons I learned was to never let my audience sense any reservation I might have. If teenagers know you are afraid they will eat you alive and take the upper hand. When I stopped and reflected there really were three major life lesson truths I learned while logging in hours instructing teens to pursue excellence in all areas of their life. So with knees occasionally knocking and heart pounding I set out to educate and spent 10 years in my classroom role as the sex mom.

Be relevant

When I get up to speak to a classroom of young energetic teens I often wonder, "What are they thinking in those not yet quite fully developed brains?" I strive to keep plugged into current issues, music, cultural norms, trendy fashion, slang language, and popular interests of young people. Several years into this teaching adventure my own teenagers became quite helpful at keeping me informed about the main stream culture. All you need to do is pay attention and not be afraid to ask questions. What kind of books are they reading? What media venue is the most successful to communicate with them? Who are their heroes? What irritates them most about their parents? What Hollywood movies rock their world? Did that belly button piercing hurt? How did you decide on that hair color? Do you find sagging pants attractive? Explain your tattoo to me?

I recall asking a young teenage boy to show me some dance moves after class one day. His classmates that surrounded us testified to his popular dancing reputation. I was sincerely intrigued. I'd be willing to bet not many "mothers" took time for a dance lesson. About a dozen students witnessed me learning some hot new dance movements with howls of laughter. I was a terrible student but they LOVED seeing me try. My interest in their world and its ways earned me access and trust to enter in. Just keeping it real went a long way to gaining their listening ears. I may not agree with what I discover and learn but in the process I have gained a boat load of information and understanding.

My journey to uncover truths about my teenage friends surprisingly transformed me into being a relevant mom. I found that I could often "sneak the spinach in" as dialogue and conversation ensued. Let me see if I can explain this. My oldest daughter Noelle is a master at sneaking vegetables into meals that her husband Chris knows nothing about! She can disguise carrots, zucchini, tomatoes, kale, onions, and my personal favorite, spinach, into her casseroles. She must have learned that trick from me as I like to mix spinach into my salads, sandwiches, quiches and lasagna. Without knowing it, spinach haters are receiving benefits and nutrients from the very thing they *think* they don't like. The big surprise to me was that a middle-aged mother of three who had been married 30+ years suddenly had a platform to communicate from. My casual and laid-back style of communication was laced with vegetables and nuggets of truth. I was able to effortlessly serve up abstinence to a classroom full of students who may have thought they didn't want to hear what I had say. I must report that not all students hung on my every word in rapt attention. Not every student stayed awake the entire time (I was famous for waking them up). Some of my earlier presentations caused me to question my ability to endure and out last and outwit the most stubborn teen. At times it felt as though I was spitting into the wind. My mentor Debbie told me to look for one heart that was changed and impacted by my visit to each class. I would pour over the after class evaluations searching for one young teen that may have been transformed that day. When I questioned why I was doing this type of education I would simply go read some of those past evaluations to encourage myself. Here are a few that touched my heart and soul.

"This guest speaker saved my life. Yes, that is exactly what you have done."

"The fluidity and impact of your presentation hits us like warm butter on soft bread. I respect the tempo and lack of scolding and negative incentive to push us the safe route. Your method is unlike the others kids have seen whether you won us all over is unknown but likely and rest assured and be proud you've won one."

"This was great. I wish I had someone to talk to about having sex before doing it. I have changed my decision and now will stay abstinent until marriage."

"This presentation helped confirm to me my choice of abstinence was the best one."

"My mom never talks about sex with me. I'm glad you did."

"Thank you so much you really touched my heart and life today you made it a fun and safe environment. I felt very good after you finished and am looking at my life very differently now. You changed my opinion."

"People have been pressuring me to have sex with my boyfriend and I was considering it. Now I am not going to even think about it!"

"You helped me to choose abstinence... Again"

"This presentation surely wasn't boring!"

And my personal favorite...

"I would give almost anything to have a mom like you Lorrie."

Gain their respect

The first thing I had to do was to make my presentation personal. A short one hour time block made that quite a challenge. I had to lay down my cards and gain their respect with the allotted classroom clock ticking. Most students were surprised at how long I had been married to my husband John. When I told them about my children, some played local sports with them. I did have the pleasure of speaking in classes that included my own children. I would begin those sessions by introducing myself as mother of their classmate who was in attendance that day. Asking for a round of applause (and a medal of honor) for my child who was allowing me to come to their school and speak to their peer group about SEX! Really…a cool mom is usually the one who is NOT your mom! After all, would they want their mother to come and speak to their friends?! Suddenly my own child was pitied by their classmates! Hopefully I also demonstrated respect.

I did have one humorous moment that involved my son Grant. I was sharing about a research study that revealed "who" was experiencing the most satisfying sex. When I revealed the answer (those who had been married 20 years and more, like me!) to the class, I suppose my son suddenly became very uncomfortable! The visual picture he had in his mind was just too much for him and he shot his hand up in class with what I thought was a question. When I called on him he said "Mom, could I please go home now!" I do believe that was one of the funniest moments of my speaking career! Just in case you wanted to know I didn't dismiss him from class that day! My oldest daughter Noelle recently wrote in a Mother's day blog about a funny memory of her mom…the sex mom.

"When I was in high school, my mother volunteered to be on the public school line up for talking to teens about sex and abstinence in health class. I was horrified when I heard her referred to as 'the sex mom'. She wore the title proudly and spared no details when presenting in my own classroom. She gave her testimony of being a

virgin when she got married and having a wonderful and satisfying sex life years later with my father! There I was, a PRODUCT of this very truth?! Little did I know how much I would look up to her later as the friend everyone feels comfortable talking to about this topic. Way to go SEX MOM! "

Teens can smell a faker or a disingenuous spirit among them so I made it very clear that I was approachable and they could ask me anything. It's easy to tell the truth. I had no motive to lie to them. I was honest and shared personal accounts of my dating and life's experiences. Most of the questions involved being married or what it was like dating in the good old days! I assured my audience that they had far more hurdles to deal with that are more challenging than I did as a young adult. The statistics are daunting. There is more peer pressure, and sexually transmitted disease now that can rob your ability to reproduce or even cost you your life. Most teenagers do not have a personal connection to HIV/AIDS, and the majority I spoke to didn't think I had a personal connection to that disease. They were wrong. I hadn't planned on having a friend who would test positive along with her husband. No one is ever prepared to hold a sobbing friend in your arms after learning that news. There isn't a training manual to teach you how to walk that road with someone you love. I will never forget returning home to my husband & kids after spending that day with my friend. I cried in the embrace of my sweet spouse who I met at 17 years old. I thanked him over and over through flowing tears for loving me so much that he never put me at risk for any disease before or during our marriage. It was a moment I relived with much emotion with every teen I could speak to. The room would get very quiet when I shared what I knew and had experienced personally with that friend who has AIDS. No self-righteous teenager who thought they wore a bullet proof vest ever challenged me when I shared my soul and looked them in the eye. I came into their school, walked on their turf, and was causing them to evaluate their personal lives. I learned that respect can dissolve quickly if they think you can't relate to them or if they think you don't care. Just showing up to talk to a room full of wide eyed young-uns (that look often the product of an energy drink for breakfast!) gave me credibility. Too many adults quit caring about them and paying attention to what matters to them. You want respect from a teen? Love love love them and assure them you care.

Just Listen

If you have known me for more than 5 minutes then you quickly learn that I am a talker! Developing and learning techniques to be a good listener was a big mountain for me to climb. As an educator with a small block of time, I felt great pressure to unload all the information I could. Exercising the discipline to make room for questions and conversation during class time had to happen. After gaining respect and honing my abilities to be relevant, the art of listening came easier. I believe there is something inherent in us that desires to be heard. I believe we have a deep need to be listened to. I would look out into the classroom of faces and remind myself, "who here doesn't want to be listened to?"

One of the biggest mistakes I made as a parent was pulling out sermons I had meticulously prepared to deliver at an inopportune time to my children. I believe panic set in as I became aware that my years, months, weeks, days, hours and moments with them were slipping away from my control. I needed to bestow my great wealth of wisdom upon my children before I no longer could. While I could wax on for hours about my opinion and thoughts, one look in my rearview mirror taught me that it was time to ask more questions and start listening.

I implemented better listening in the classroom. Immediately they started asking questions. Often times the questions went like this: Where did I purchase those pink tennis shoes? How many kids do you have? What do you do for a living? How did you tell your boyfriend you didn't want to have sex before marriage? How long had I been married and did I like being married? That is the question that always surprised me the most! About half of these students had no clue what a healthy loving marriage relationship even looked like. Do they have questions they would like to ask, but may uncomfortable asking? Hmmm, maybe I need to answer the questions they haven't even thought to ask! Are they bored and put off by our remarks about abstinence or are they encouraged? How often my heart ached for the students who would bravely talk to me after class about their problems. I placed my arm around a young girl as she cried with grief and fear for her circumstances. They disclosed difficult relationships and were paralyzed by fear. One common thread that all teenagers have is fear of their parents and their potential reaction to a mess they got themselves into. As I learned to listen with confidence I discovered the regrets of painful dysfunctional relationships, sexually transmitted diseases, pregnancies and abortion. Instead of experiencing love, so many teens were lacking in hope. If they only knew how much we cared and prayed for those hours spent within their various classrooms. What I initially thought was a feeble attempt to assist young people in making good decisions that would last them a lifetime, turned out to be a passion that rewarded me with living my life of no regrets. My greatest joy and accomplishment was seeing the hundreds that listened and the many in response who raised their personal bar of excellence and joined me.

It was a lot of fun. It was never dull. And I don't regret one day, one hour or minute or fraction of time spent being the sex mom.

Chapter 10

Seasoned By Many

"Though one may be overpowered, two can defend themselves. A cord of three strands is not quickly broken." Ecclesiastes 4:12

I love to cook and have discovered there are many seasonings that enhance your food creation. I have also learned through some massive failures that some seasonings are simply not a good choice for your family dinner table. When my children were dating I emphasized the importance of resolving to be a stronger person during and after dating that boy/girl. Their task was to engender that person to surpass who they were before the relationship began. I'd like to think I've had that seasoning or perfume effect on others that lingered in their life. There are certainly a host of individuals who have transacted that in my sphere. I'm indebted to them for leaving a spice of life with me that seasoned my little life's meal! I share with you a few examples of those who seasoned my life and made it more flavorful,

I've often thought that I am my own worst enemy. Especially when I think I can do it by myself. It's often easier to not ask for help and instead try to power through in our own strength. I learned the fallacy of that belief after I had major surgery when I was 40 years old. I was told by the doctor I would need six weeks of rest. My two closest girlfriends, Carol and Laurie, rallied to my aid. Ahhh yes… girlfriends. (That was a lesson my husband learned… he could never be for me, my girlfriend. That is a chapter for *his* book.) My girlfriend, Laurie always keeps track of my life for me. For example, she will recall "That happened just after you had your 2nd child later that year when your hair was shorter with the bad perm. Remember?" Now why can't I remember, but she can? I love that I have cherished friends who pay more attention to me than I do.

Recently I was recovering from knee surgery and was asked what wisdom I was gleaning during my rehabilitation. This was my reflection.

I have gained valuable insight to others with this knee adventure…

I think the biggest thing is that I'm surprised that those with the least amount of time, least amount of money, and those going through the most stressful times in their life are the ones who are most inclined to reach out to assist and be helpful to me. What a blessing to interact with those who understand need, pain and suffering and freely offer love, meals, visits, icing machines and prayer to you. I am so humbled and in awe of that kind of witness in the midst of their personal trials. I find it so interesting how those I thought I might count on, were seemingly absent. As I learned before…our expectations are almost always incorrect, so it is often better not to have expectations so as not to be disappointed! That has helped me immensely not to feel "let down" by the "absent" ones. One set of friends who are in the midst of such trial and difficulty stopped by Sunday with an orchid and to check on me. Such a kind gesture that I could see gave them relief within their brokenness. The love they gave me was worth twice as much in my mind. Another friend's son wrecked her car and his substance addiction landed him in jail Friday night. She has no money to help him and her job that keeps the family afloat has important duties this week. Yet she calls to check on me... .

Another friend has a brain tumor they can't operate on until they fix other more serious problems and he dug out an icing machine from his shed from previous surgeries like mine. He and his wife delivered it to my house so it was waiting for me after surgery...they included an anniversary card with remembering my surgery day was our 32nd anniversary. They even included cheerful funny instructions for operating the machine. Their present life and circumstances were ANYTHING but that. I have a friend who has been at the Mayo Clinic in Minneapolis for the past month suffering and the doctors have no clue as to why she has lost 40 lbs and is gravely ill. She prays for me and sends me Facebook messages to encourage...me. She encourages ME?! These precious saints are teaching me. I think I will call what I'm receiving ...peace amidst the pieces.

Just hanging up someone else's wet mittens can abundantly impact an individual for life.

I have to tell you about Dora, Al & Emma, Clare Lennox, Roland & Joyce & Elinor. They are my favorite golden-seasoners.

Back in the 70's in high school I met a delightful, chatty, warm, and loving woman named Dora who sat next to me at a Billy Graham Crusade. Upon our first greeting neither one of us could stop talking. She captured my heart with her joy and laughter and with nearly everything that came out of her mouth. This was the first time I had really spent quality time with a widow in her older years. Her zeal for life was contagious and we became fast friends. I visited her for many years in her retirement home. We spoke of marriage, faith and friendship. Dora gave me an intimate peek into her world of senior living. She modeled for me a lifestyle of love and busyness for others. Every Christmas I hang a handmade gold beaded bell on our tree that she gave me as a gift for being her special friend. That bell has always represented and will always remind me of the kind of friend I should be no matter what age I am.

Have you ever received a gift that was too big for you to handle? Two extraordinary people from my church befriended me in high school during a time when I was making big decisions about my future. When I met this sweet elderly couple, Al and Emma, I surmised quickly that they were losing faith in young people of my generation. They seemed intrigued with me since I seemed to have half a brain on my youthful shoulders, was not too boy crazy, and was propelling myself in a positive direction with the fear of God on my heart. Maybe I represented hope and confidence that our generation were not all headed to hell in a hand basket! We became friends and spent time together. Understanding my family could never afford to pay for college education, Al & Emma lovingly and privately offered to pay for my education at a private out-of-state Christian college. The generosity from this kind and loving couple was overwhelming to me. It took weeks of weighing, discussing, mulling and praying for me to come to a decision that would have a colossal effect on my life and future. The gift and gesture was just too sizable for my heart to handle, so I humbly and gratefully declined. It is absolutely the largest charitable offering I have ever received. I am self-assured that I made the right decision as I probably and most likely would not have continued dating and later marry my husband. Al and Emma patterned for me to give hilariously when you are prompted to do so. Give and love and don't hold back. Just this morning I elected to wear a mother of pearl cross necklace that was given to me by these cherished comrades. It was a gift to me after they returned from a holy land visit to Israel. I have treasured it and remembered our friendship upon wearing it. I didn't realize that hours later my mother would call from my hometown to tell me of Emma's passing at age 97. I felt a swelling in my throat as I remembered these kind generous individuals. The tears inspire me now to be a giver and follow in their steps in mentoring others. I believe I've got some big boots to fill.

Potential adventure awaits you at every turn, but you don't usually see it coming in the form of an elderly woman sitting near the bike trail frantically waving at my friend and I as we rode bikes one day near my home. This spry white haired wiry widowed woman had fallen and suspected she hurt her hip. She couldn't move. She was smart to stay put and I was impressed with her wisdom immediately. I stayed with her while my friend rode ahead and called an ambulance to aid my new friend Clare. As the EMT wheeled her away I slipped my phone number into her hand. She told me she had no family locally so I offered to help her in any way I could. A week later she phoned from her hospital room to report on her condition and thank me for "rescuing her".

She frequently referred to that circumstance that brought us into a unique friendship that would span almost 18 years. She effortlessly poured into my life all that embodied simplicity. She taught me crafts in her tiny retirement home apartment. Crafts that were print impressions of mushroom spores that we preserved with hair spray! Clare instructed me how to enjoy banana boats for an upcoming camping trip with my family. Slice a banana length-wise while in the skin and stuff in chocolate chips and marshmallows and then wrap in foil and throw it into the coals of the campfire for a few minutes! She taught me about gardening and then nurtured me and her potted planted on her tiny patio. She shared propagated plants and seeds with me for my own garden. One time while visiting my home she declared that the plants were growing to mutant proportion in my yard! She made me feel like a master gardener. She shared with me her bird watching journal and notations of which birds returned and when they arrived to her feeder. She was passionate about her little feathered friends and chatted cheerfully about the ornithological technical names she knew. On occasion I brought her bird seed as a gift to keep the local sparrows happy. She never knew how much I disliked birds (thanks to Alfred Hitchcock's- The Birds which scared the stuffing out of me). I could never bring myself to reveal that guarded secret to her since I know it would spoil the joy she had sharing her feathered friends with me. Clare grew up in a generation that saved everything! Little strings, ribbons, cards, and paper that was then recycled and designed into "new" creations. She taught me simple ways to stretch a dime on a fixed budget. For her birthday in December I would bring her ripe persimmons which she cherished and her smile alone was thanks enough. I had never tasted persimmons and her tales of enjoying them as a child persuaded me to venture out more in the produce department when shopping. I trimmed her hair regularly and moved her winter clothes around for her. We found plenty to chat about as she recalled her travels in the Orient as a young woman in the 1930's. A precious treasure I own is a bell from that trip she unselfishly gave to me for a haircut. Clare always insisted on settling with me for the haircuts. I insisted on no pay so she figured out schemes to even the score.

I believe I was the one who received far more from our precious friendship but she would vehemently argue it was she who redeemed more since I "rescued her from peril when she broke her hip"...ahhh yes, She would not let me forget I saved her life! Parades and school concerts of my children passed with the years and soon my visits with her were during the daytime school hours. I recall the day and moment I discerned that she didn't remember my recent visit. I quizzed her and reminded her but she adamantly said I hadn't visited that day and she wondered why. It was confusing to me and alerted me to mental and health changes that were taking place. The episodes of forgetting and not remembering were becoming more frequent. I started to write my visits on her calendar in my handwriting with a smiley face so she could recall them later. Unfortunately calendars began to mean nothing and she would ask me what day it was. It broke my heart to arrive, greet, then leave on an errand for her, only to return to have her greet me as though she hadn't seen me in 6 months (but it had only been 30 minutes). I remember telling a friend how congenial she was every single time my face came through the door even though the shadow of passing minutes would cause Clare to forget. A valued gift God gave me was that she never forgot who I was during her decline and eventual passing. She would fail to remember the day of the week, and what she ate for lunch but even dementia could not rob her of her loving friendship with me. She loved little ole me…Lorrie, who rescued an old lady… who stumbled and fell while walking home. Love grew and arrived in a most uncanny way and I purposed that I would someday grow up to be just like Clare.

Another dear saintly woman who got inserted into our life when we bought our second home was our perky neighbor Elinor. The thing I loved most about Elinor was that she told me I always made her laugh. She was entertained and tickled by just about everything I said. Now that is the kind of neighbor you want. That is the kind of friend I desired too! Find me delightful and funny and I'm your friend for life! She was a kind woman who found innovative ways to spoil my children. This silver saint took a vested interest in my children and lovingly taught them valuable life lessons.

Our oldest daughter grew quickly into her teens but in later years enjoyed our neighbor in our home for meals. She was a very good cook and homemaker so she had tales to tell about her own family from yesteryear. She took special care to inquire about her boyfriend, her high school activities and busy social life. One prom she floated over with her date to give Elinor a personal viewing of her fine dress and handsome date complete with corsage. It delighted her to no end and she would speak of it for months to come.

Each year our family sang Christmas carols for some of the elderly neighbors during the holiday season. Elinor was the one neighbor who kept a box of Sees candy ready for our arrival and anticipated performance each year. She also kept a bright kelly-green colored glass bowl full of candy to reward my son for pulling weeds, taking out the garbage, or helping her with a chore. More often he would just show up at her door to inquire about a job when he was bored with his sisters. She never gave him candy for just showing up and being cute. She bought candy for that bowl that HE liked. Not her favorites, but his and ok, maybe a few peppermint chocolate patties for me found their way in there since she coerced that information out of me. Truth is I didn't realize she was doing it until 15 years into sharing fences! Oh yes, our "let's go 50/50 on it together" crooked fence we built with her blessing. We did not realize the granite boulders buried beneath the ground prohibited us from constructing it in a straight line on the property boundary! She laughed and thought it was funny.

Our middle child and daughter Whitney was mesmerized by this elderly woman's fascination with dolls. Her home was well stocked with an enviable doll collection. Whitney asked her if she thought she would ever be too old for dolls. Elinor confirmed that she was old but she hadn't out grown her dolls! She invited Whitney over to "play" and visit with her dolls whenever she wanted to. I'd repeatedly have to wander back to retrieve dolly lover Whitney from Elinors' house after several hours to give the woman a break. She was charmed by our daughter and assured us the pleasure was alllllllll hers. One particular doll named "Pussy Cat," with pink dress and brown coiffed hair, enraptured our daughter's tender spirit and one day Elinor asked if Whitney would baby doll sit her for a few hours while she was away on errands. Whitney was more than tickled pink to say yes and assured Elinor she would entertain and watch over that doll with intentional dedicated passion! Several hours later Elinor showed up on the door step and asked for the doll back. I recall that Whitney, who never put the doll down once and gave it her full attention, dutifully handed over Pussy Cat to her rightful owner. The next day Elinor invited her to repeat baby doll sitting only this time it was for all afternoon. Once again she summoned Whitney to return the doll and they exchanged doll details about their wild afternoon adventure together. The next day Elinor asked Whitney if she'd like to take the doll for a sleepover. Holy mackerel and heck yes she would! It brings to mind Whitney asking me that afternoon (with the doll permanently attached to her hip) if I thought Elinor might give the doll to her one day? After all she had so many many dolls and how could one woman possibly find time to play with and enjoy such a vast collection!? I didn't know the answer to that question but my interest was piqued as to what my feisty fascinating neighbor might be up to! The next day when Whitney returned the doll, Elinor told her what a lovely job she did caring for it. She said she had to be sure she would love and show guardianship before asking her if the doll could live at our home permanently. I cherished that moment as I saw how this wise woman taught responsibility to my daughter.

One of the activities I helped my neighbor with was errands, doctor appointments and shopping. A piece of advice that I learned from my friend Laurie was to not hurry my 90+ year old friend. I preferred to let her think that I had all the time in the world at the grocery store. One particular afternoon we strolled through the grocery store at a snail's pace. I assured her we had lots time to shop though. As we turned the corner our basket bumped in to another shopper. To her surprise, she collided with an old friend from her church that she had not seen for a long time. Her friend was overjoyed to see her and they picked up a lively conversation. That was my cue to head to the produce section for some of my garden favorites. When I moseyed back to her side in the meat department, I remarked at how lovely it was for her to reconnect with an old friend. With a slight smirk and giggle, she announced that her friend probably thought she was dead! So she was probably REALLY happy to see her on this side of the green grass. Elinor was always saying funny things like that. My most memorable adventure with her involved a shopping incident at Costco.

After loading our basket for an hour, we were standing in line to check out when I looked over my shoulder. She was slumping to one side and appeared to have a seizure. While I supported her, an off duty fireman came to my aid and together we eased her to the cold concrete floor. Minutes later when she came back with full sensibility, she called out my name and asked me why she was laying on the floor at Costco! With fear and trembling (and quite loud) vocals, I told her I had not a clue why she would choose that particular place to pass out on me. An EMT unit arrived quickly to transport her to our local hospital. I remained at her side while they ran tests, and poked and prodded looking for answers. I told her that one thing was for sure. She brought new meaning to the phrase "shop till you drop!" I announced that I would never take her shopping at Costco again... And I never did.

Elinor liked to treat me to lunch as payment for my time and gas. We had our favorites and Chinese food was regularly at the top of the list. She actually preferred Denny's since it had a senior discount menu. I didn't catch on at first, but she would always ask me what I was going to order. I'd mention one or two things that looked interesting and when it came time to order she would have one of the menu items I had mentioned. It happened every single time. Weeks later I finally called her out on it and asked her why she did that and she told me that she had misplaced her glasses and was too embarrassed to admit it. She was struggling to read everything! We made her an appointment that afternoon to have an eye exam and get new glasses ordered so she could see...and order for herself at

Denny's again. Her sweet quirky pride touched me. She didn't want to bother or ever put me out to assist her. I pray I told her often that such was never the case and the pleasure was mine as I learned from this lovely woman.

The idea of spending a week alone with my parents in Montana while my husband stayed home in California with our 3 children seemed like a good trade. I rarely got my parents to myself with 4 other siblings or my family in tow to compete for time with. A leisurely week sounded fun and relaxing to me. I think I had my bags packed 2 weeks before my scheduled flight and that made my family question my motives for leaving them all alone. The concerns were vocal and loud. Our son was worried no one would feed him in my absence, but I was more concerned about who would feed the dog?! One daughter truly believed her dad would have an emotional breakdown and the other was sure she would turn into Cinderella doing housework for everyone. Funny, I was only worried about the dog. A couple of days before I arrived my dad phoned me and excitedly said Mac and Joyce were going to be visiting while I was there and he was anxious for me to meet them. After all they were amazing fabulous people! Uh oh, there goes the alone time I dreamed of.

I had heard my father speak lovingly of his Vietnam buddy over the years. Mac did this and Mac did that, and oh Mac and I got ourselves into trouble doing this and that. They were inseparable during their tour in 1966-68 but after returning stateside they lost contact and years, yes, numerous years passed before the age of the internet enabled Roland (Mac) to search, find and contact his long lost friend. I was not prepared for what I experienced when I met this lovely couple.

Roland and my father had a bond that I had never seen him share with any man before. They were like brothers. He was a long lost best friend. Mac was a buddy through thick and thin. I remember laughing at them while they were in the yard cleaning, counting, comparing and preparing their trout catch for picture taking after a morning of fishing together. They acted like a couple of school chums poking and making fun of each other like junior high boys fresh with freckles and wide grins. Joyce and mom were constantly rolling their eyes but loving every second of this new chapter of friendship. Those old men were certainly making up for lost years! I never laughed as much as I did hanging out with Roland & Joyce that week. I fell hard in love with them! I secretly watched them all interact and decided it was a love and friendship circle that I wanted to emulate for myself. I want to love and be loved like that! I watched my dad tearfully say goodbye to his dear friend as their motor home pulled away. I stood there trying to stop the flow from my eyes alongside both of my parents. Who had I just met that won me over from the top of my head to my toes?! I'm going to need my family to meet this charming couple!

The following summer when we traveled to Florida's Disneyworld as a family I insisted that we plan a visit with Mac and Joyce, but we would call them Roland and Joyce. Mac was my father's name for him and I couldn't quite bring myself to call him by that name since it seemed sacred to those veteran soldiers. My family fell in love with

Roland & Joyce as I knew they would. We planned to stay one night with them but ended up coming back and staying another. We went on an everglade airboat ride and visited their favorite eatery shack with all their former Harley riding buddies. Wait a minute … Harley riding friends? They both used to ride and even though they didn't ride anymore they were entirely comfortable in that environment. Roland took daughter Whitney out on the open air dance floor and referred to her as his granddaughter. He approached several toothless, leathered, tanned and tattooed men for photos on a few of their "hogs" for Whitney in the parking area. Everyone treated this couple with dignity and respect. We were way out of our neighborhood hanging out there. But the gator tail, frog legs, grouper and chicken lunch was as unforgettable as Roland and Joyce would be.

They traveled to attend daughter Whitney's wedding in our hometown. We seated them as grandparents and special guests as they earned the title "family". Joyce taught us a phrase we all giggled about and still use. If a group got to chatting too aggressively and bordered on gossip about someone then the rule was you jump in and say, "But ____ sure is a good swimmer!" It was code for enough negative talk about this person and let's move on. It's always a good laugh to use it when others have no clue but to imagine that the person really is a good swimmer. I learned to be a soul with kindness, love and respect for one another. I will also never ever be a fuddy duddy. (Whatever that is.)

Joyce just passed away into the arms of her Jesus unexpectedly this spring. We miss her. Her scent of loveliness lingers in our lives. I want to leave that scent behind for others as a life well lived.

I want to live a life of no regrets. Love with my whole heart. Learn for a lifetime and never forget my first lesson of wet mittens. As I wrote this book and compiled my personal stories I realized I still have many more tales to tell. I don't believe my life lessons are going to end any time soon so I'm sharing some of them in my blog you can read at: http://wetmittens.blogspot.com/

May your mittens be dry, warm and cozy!

10793771R00067

Made in the USA
San Bernardino, CA
25 April 2014